1. The Painting Process	1
2. Coloring in the Lines	5
3. Undesirable Hues	9
4. Artistic Influences	14
5. Bleeding Colors	22
6. Hidden Layers	38
7. Doubting the Process	48
8. Design Adjustments	57
9. Emerging Beauty	65
10. God's Techniques	72
11. Finding the Master Painter	79
12. Accessing the Savior's Palette	85
13. Eternal Rules of Composition	94
14. Embracing God's Methods	102
15. Savoring the Creative Process	108
16. Just Enough Paint	115
17. Depth Through Shadows	119
18. Angelic Luster	127
19. Artistic Interpretation	135
20. Adding Dimension	141
21. His Masterpiece	146
Afterword	153
Citations	163

Copyright © 2022 - Tangled Willow Press

This material is neither made, provided, approved, nor endorsed by Intellectual Reserve, Inc. or The Church of Jesus Christ of Latter-day Saints. Any content or opinions expressed, implied or included in or with the material are solely those of the owner and not those of Intellectual Reserve, Inc. or The Church of Jesus Christ of Latter-day Saints.

Cover Design: Poole Publishing Services
Cover painting: Marie Gray
Editor: Charissa Stastny
ISBN: 978-1-948861-28-1

For Tyson, Jacob, Sierra, Spencer, Malea, & Kayla,
You gave me reason to find the beauty in the shadows.

Brushstrokes of *Grace*

Becoming God's Masterpiece Through Chronic Illness

Marie Gray

1

THE PAINTING PROCESS

Has your life ever felt like a jumbled mess of paint splatters and chaotic scribbles? Despite your best efforts to place specific colors just where you want them, do you feel like you have no control of the ugly hues that have emerged? Has the picture-perfect life you imagined become unrecognizable due to trials you have encountered? Maybe infertility, divorce, or losing a loved one has altered the life you envisioned. Maybe chronic illness, anxiety, or depression has made your plans impossible to carry out. Do those unwanted brushstrokes of your life's painting make you wish you could start over with a new canvas?

If so, I hope my story will help you not feel alone and discouraged. My deepest hope is that my story will encourage you to trust in God's process. With all your heart! He is the Master Painter. Only He knows how to transform us into exquisite works of art. What seems like haphazard brushstrokes and bleak shadows to us now will come together someday, through the grace of Jesus Christ, to create something more exquisite than we could have ever imagined when we exercise faith and allow Him access to our hearts.

Artists take steps while painting that may not make sense to those with a limited understanding of the overall creative process. For that reason, as an artist myself, I do not like people seeing the beginning stages of my painting. I start out doing things that do not make sense to those who are not aware of the methods that I have envisioned and prepared.

When people see the painting early on, I have to say, "Don't worry! It is going to turn out. It looks strange right now, but it will look better in the end."

For example, to make a painting look more cohesive, I repeat colors. If I put yellow in the background, I put that same yellow in any other place that I can detect a hint of yellow. If someone saw me putting yellow on the face and in the clothes of the subject, they might wonder what in the world I was doing, but an artist knows it will unify the subject with the background.

Another thing I do is add complementary colors to shadows to give them more substance than just adding gray or black. Complementary colors are two colors that are opposite of each other on the color wheel. Examples of this are red and green, blue and orange, and purple and yellow. When a pair of complementary colors are placed next to each other, they create the highest contrast, and the colors appear intensified.

On the other hand, when mixed together, they create a neutral gray. If I painted green in the shadows of a red area of a painting, an onlooker might assume it would make it look bad. In reality, adding the complementary color makes a beautiful and natural shadow. The artist knows that details which seem *strange*, in the end make a painting more cohesive, brilliant, and full of life.

The Lord knows trials that do not make sense to us are necessary to add depth and meaning to our souls. I can see Him saying, "Don't worry! I know the process does not make sense right now, but you lack understanding of all that I have envisioned for you to become. The results will astonish you."

We need to trust that OUR Creator knows how to make a masterpiece out of the brushstrokes of our lives.

Life often takes different turns than we expect, and we face trials that cause agony and heartache. We need to have faith that He, who knows all, knows how to create something beautiful out of those unexpected brushstrokes. He knows our divine potential, and we need to trust that His method and process will have results far greater than anything we could ever foresee or create for ourselves. The process can be difficult and painful, but it will be worth it.

Doctrine and Covenants 122:7 says, "All these things shall give thee experience, and shall be for thy good."

From a young age, I had my life mapped out. I was excited to accomplish great things through hard work and discipline. I knew life would involve trials, but I was confident that they would be ones I could handle and that would make me a stronger person.

Then I faced trials that made me feel weak and useless. I thought trials were supposed to make me a better person, but the trials I confronted felt like a hindrance to my progression, not a help. I felt that the trials were keeping me from becoming the person I wanted to be. These brushstrokes seemed out of place.

Why would God let those hideous colors into my painting?

Now I know, through hindsight, that tribulations which do not make sense mold us in ways that we often cannot see or understand when we choose faith over bitterness. When we place our will on the altar, and trust our Creator to make more of our lives than we can on our own, then amazing things happen through His grace.

The Atonement of Jesus Christ encompasses much more than the forgiveness of our sins. His grace is divine help that we can access each day, making us more capable in all aspects of our lives. His Atonement does not simply assist us–it changes us.

He can perfect our spiritual paintings, adding colors that are more splendid and effulgent than are available on our own limited palettes. It is through the grace of Jesus Christ that our trials transform each of us into His transcendent masterpiece if we have faith, accept His will, and follow Him.

2

COLORING IN THE LINES

*A*s the third of six children, I had a hefty dose of middle-child syndrome. I thought my two older sisters got all the privileges and that my two younger sisters and brother received all the attention, so I tried to make myself known. Whether I was battling it out in a game of Monopoly at home or competing for the best grades at school, I wanted to come out on top. My driven and competitive spirit spilled out into many parts of my life, in both positive and negative ways.

In elementary school, I loved coloring contests, and my first-grade teacher held them frequently for our class. She would give everyone the same picture to color, and then the class would vote on the best one. I wanted so badly to be victorious, so I worked with great effort to meticulously stay in the lines. I won almost every time, and it brought me immense satisfaction.

A friend told me later about a comical incident that evolved during one of those coloring contests. Apparently, she and a group of our classmates got tired of me winning the contests, so they secretly devised a plan to beat me. They decided to copy my technique of coloring with heavy, dark strokes. After they finished copying my usual technique, they sneaked over to see how my picture was looking.

Surprisingly, I had changed my method that day and had colored the picture very lightly. Realizing mine looked better than theirs, they quickly decided to improvise. Each of them grabbed scissors and used the sharp edge to scrape the heavy colors off their papers so theirs would look more like mine. She told of their frustration when, despite their clever plans, I once again came out triumphant. I had no idea at the time that my accomplishment that brought me such satisfaction was disappointing and annoying to my classmates.

My desire to succeed also affected the way I played sports. Because of my ambition, I put in long hours to improve. Basketball was my favorite sport, and you could often find me shooting the ball on our hoop outside. The saying, "you can do anything you set your mind to," was a huge driving force for me, and I yearned to work hard in hopes of becoming a basketball star. Recently, I was reminiscing with one of my cousins, and his main memory of me was of me shooting foul shot after foul shot on our driveway. I was determined to put the work in to accomplish my dreams.

I tried to take advantage of any opportunity to improve my basketball skills. My dad used to play basketball in the mornings at our community gym before work with some friends, and I loved to tag along and practice my skills on the other court while they played. Even if it meant dragging myself out of bed at six in the morning in the winter while it was still dark and freezing outside, I enjoyed the time to practice and spend time with my dad. I have a vivid memory of one of those mornings, dribbling fast up and down the court, practicing my right- and left-handed layups.

After my dad finished playing with his friends, he came over to my side of the gym and gave me tips on how to improve my form as I did layup after layup. I relished the attention, and I gained immense satisfaction from developing my skills.

I also soaked in any advice my dad gave me at the end of my basketball games. I listened closely, mentally planning how to execute the plays better based on his suggestions. Now that I am older, I can see that my reaction to those critiques was a little abnormal. Most children react negatively and get defensive when their parents analyze their performance. In contrast, I saw those critiques as the means to become a better player.

Similarly, I gleaned from my dad's expertise when I watched college basketball games with him. He would point out what made the plays successful or how they could have been carried out better. I enjoyed being by my dad's side, figuring out different strategies.

I also sought out everyday activities that would increase my athleticism. Many children are out riding their bikes for fun. Although I did that as well, I also remember riding my bike as a training tool for sports. I often tried to get as good of a workout as possible to increase my strength and stamina. We have a road near my childhood home that goes up a steep hill, and I remember taking that road many times on my bike to try to get to the top without stopping. It was truly a test of endurance, but I loved the exhilaration of working hard to get to the top.

I would often try to convince one of my siblings to join me on the ride, which always made it more fun. One reward for this workout was getting to ride down the hill at the end.

Although we picked up so much speed that it did not feel safe at times, it was an amazing feeling to go so fast that the air pushed against our faces. The best reward was being able to have a good start to my sports seasons, having built up lots of endurance and being able to run and run without any trouble. It made me feel invincible.

That same determination also came into play when I joined the track team in high school. I was not the fastest runner, but I did well at distance running because I had the stamina to run for a long time. I was lucky to have amazing parents who supported me. In the summertime, I wanted to train and improve, so my mom would wake me early in the morning to go running before it got too hot outside. She would drive me to the high school track, and I would run laps while she walked. My parents also drove me to several 5K fun runs in nearby cities to help me train. It made me feel special to have my parents so invested in my success.

I had a good work ethic, and I thought that was all I needed to create a happy life. I believed I could do anything I set my mind to, and I did not foresee anything getting in the way of all my dreams coming true. I believed that if I put in the work with determination, I could accomplish my heart's desires. I thought I had control of my destiny.

I assumed I just needed to diligently keep coloring within the lines, and my life's artwork would come out just like I planned. In reality, no amount of work ethic or drive would be able to fix or even ease the trials looming on my horizon. My tenacious spirit would have to learn to deal with feeling vanquished in ways over which I had no control.

3

UNDESIRABLE HUES

*I*n my artistic endeavors of youth, I learned that when I contained the colors, I was able to make a neat and tidy product just like I wanted. If I stayed within the lines with my preferred hues, I was pleased with the results. Toward the end of high school, I learned that sometimes it did not matter how disciplined I was at keeping my life's colors where I wanted them. Somehow, undesirable hues entered the design I had planned out.

Those unwanted colors started to find their way into my life during the track season of my junior year. I already had two successful seasons of track under my belt, and I felt prepared for the next season, due to lots of hard work and training.

Unfortunately, I started that season having just gotten over a bad case of bronchitis. I assumed that, although it was a rough beginning, my body would heal quickly, and success would come. But things ended up going downhill. Probably because of the lingering effects of bronchitis, I started having asthma attacks whenever I ran hard. I had never had any breathing issues before, so it made me feel crippled to not have my lungs work as normal.

I was not about to let this new issue ruin my track season, so I pushed through it as much as possible. I remember at my first couple of races, I was able to finish my races, but after crossing the finish line I had an extremely hard time catching my breath. It was scary. I remember trying to walk it off as I held my hands over my chest, gasping for air and wheezing.

My mom was right by my side during one of my worst asthma attacks, and she panicked as she watched me struggle to take each breath as I paced back and forth. Fortunately, I slowly regained my ability to breathe, avoiding an emergency. I left those races feeling defeated by my body. I hated feeling a total lack of control of my breathing and of the situation.

After my mom saw me in such a precarious state, she decided I should see a doctor. The doctor diagnosed me with exercise-induced asthma and prescribed a preventative inhaler to take each day before I ran to inhibit the attacks. I was so excited to have an easy fix for my problem.

Unfortunately, it was not the solution I hoped it would be. I used the prescribed inhaler each day before I ran, and my body did not react well to the medication. It instantly made me feel weak and shaky, and I could not run without feeling jittery and sickly.

I did not know which was worse, having asthma attacks when I ran, or using an inhaler that took away all my vitality. I do not remember much about that season. I do know I tried to stick it out, thinking that with time the inhaler would not make me feel so horrible. It was so hard to not be my energetic, hard-working self. I could not just push through like I was used to doing.

The only other thing I vividly remember from that track

season was my race at Districts. It was my chance to get to State in the two-mile race. I took my preventative inhaler beforehand so my asthma would not be an issue, but once again my body had a negative reaction to it. As soon as the race started, I could tell something was not right. My body felt so weak and shaky. It is hard to explain exactly how it felt, but it was so painful to run, like my body was screaming at me to stop, though I did not want to do so.

I had eight laps to run, which felt impossible since even the first lap nearly killed me. I remember struggling to make it around each lap of the track and praying to be able to finish the race. It was obvious that I would not be winning that race or even placing, but I did not want to be a quitter with my coach and all my teammates watching.

The thing I remember most about that race was passing my biggest cheerleaders, my parents, on the sidelines as I struggled to put one leg in front of the other. During those difficult laps, my parents clearly saw the severe pain I was in by my facial expressions and jerky stride. I heard my mom yelling from the stands, "Stop, Marie! Just stop!" I could sense the panic and concern in her voice. Watching me suffer was killing her.

I passed by them and continued to finish my sixth lap. Her voice echoed in my mind as I started around the seventh lap, "Stop Marie! Just Stop!"

The pain and fatigue overwhelmed me, and I knew that my mom was right. I needed to stop. When total exhaustion took over near the end of the seventh lap, my mom's loving words gave me the courage to stop running.

Quitting was the hardest thing I had ever done. I stumbled off the track into the center field of grass. Total disappointment set in. I felt like I had done all I could to make my track season successful and had failed. As I walked off the field, I tried to hold back tears. I was already a quitter, and I did not want to be a cry-baby, too. My parents and friends consoled me. I don't know if they knew how upset and defeated I really felt, but their kindness meant the world to me.

I watched the rest of the meet with a big lump in my throat. I could not wait to get back home so I could let my emotions free and sob into my pillow. It felt like the longest meet and the longest drive home with me desperately trying to keep my emotions in check when I felt like my world had collapsed around me.

For the first time in my life, I felt like I did not have control of my circumstances. I reflected on the motivational quotes I had heard in the past, like, "You can do anything you put your mind to," and I became cynical and angry. *No, that is not true*, I thought. There is no way I could have had a successful track season. I tried my hardest, and I still could not reach my goals. I became resentful of the people who had made me think I could do anything.

There are some things we really cannot do, no matter our mindset.

This was a turning point. My health was never the same after that, although the symptoms at first only manifested when I pushed too hard physically. Sports, one of my greatest joys, became not only difficult but probably not healthy for me. My body was telling me not to push so hard.

When my senior year rolled around, I decided to try to still play sports. Volleyball was not an issue because it never pushed me to the breaking point physically, but my basketball season was extremely difficult. My competitiveness got me through, but it was frustrating that things that were once easy for me became a major ordeal. I remember feeling sick from my inhaler as I tried to hustle on the court and play tough defense.

I especially remember one game where we were down to the wire, and I felt horrible as I struggled to keep the person I was guarding from getting the ball. I do not remember how the game turned out—I just remember how horrible I felt and how hard it was to push through. I felt so defeated after that game, not by the other team but by my own body.

Why didn't my body work correctly anymore?

I half-heartedly made the decision not to do track that year. I was so uncertain of my decision that I still went to the team meeting at the beginning of the season, hoping I would feel impressed to change my mind. After much thought, I realized my body was now incapable of distance running, no matter how much I wanted to make it work. The races that were once my forte were now impossible for my body. I was so sad to miss out on my final season. I hated feeling out of control of my situation, but this had become my reality.

My expectation of being able to create my artwork the way I wanted remained unfulfilled. Disappointing colors entered my canvas, no matter how hard I tried to regulate the hues.

Little did I know, this brief experience was only a small taste of the extreme challenges I would later face that would leave me feeling powerless. Tones that were unappealing to me would inevitably become part of my life's artwork.

4

ARTISTIC INFLUENCES

Most artists are impacted by the style and technique of artists that came before them. Those artistic influences leave a lasting impression, shaping artists' views, and impacting the artists' goals of what they want to achieve through their own creative process.

As an art student, I enjoyed learning about art history and gleaning from skillful artists of the past. Similarly, in my life's pursuits, there were people I sought to learn from and emulate. The two greatest influences in my life, who shaped my goals and aspirations, were my parents. I wanted to follow their artistic style because of the exquisite composition they created.

My dad was the epitome of hard work and dedication. Whenever he had a job or responsibility, he completed it to the best of his ability. Whether it was at work, fulfilling his callings at church, or in his duties as a husband and father, he fulfilled each role with meticulous attention to detail.

Despite work and church requiring much of his time and

attention, he made family a priority. It meant the world to me when he would rush over after work meetings to see at least part of my basketball or volleyball games at the high school. Somehow, I always noticed when he would walk into the gym and either make his way to the stands or stay close to the gym entrance to see as much of the game as possible. It meant even more to me knowing the extra effort it took for him to see me play.

Another way he fit me into his schedule was by joining me at school lunch sometimes when I was in elementary school. I felt like the coolest kid in school when I was waiting in the lunch line and saw my dad walking toward me. It felt like having a superhero coming to join me at lunch with my friends. Sometimes I would be oblivious to him walking toward me, and the kids in my class would start tapping me on the shoulder and pointing his way, saying excitedly, "Your dad is here!" I felt so special to have all my classmates just as excited as me that my dad was there.

My dad did not have much time for hobbies, but fishing was an activity he loved and sometimes squeezed into his schedule. I am sure taking us children along made things more complicated, but we appreciated his efforts to create bonding memories with us.

Sometimes he would take a couple of us camping under the stars the night before a planned fishing day. In the morning, in order for him to start fishing as early as possible without waking us up, he put life jackets on us when we were still in our sleeping bags, picked us up in our sleeping bags, and put us in the fishing boat with him. After getting a little more sleep, my sibling and I would wake up in the small, aluminum boat, rocking peacefully in the middle of the lake, with the smell of nature all around us. Then we got up and indulged in the much-anticipated gas station food, and fished the day away. Fishing with my dad was a sweet memory because his love for us was so apparent as he made the extra effort to include us in such a unique experience.

My dad was probably overwhelmed at times as he tried to balance his busy schedule while also making time for his family, but he seemed to do it flawlessly. I got used to hearing people tell me how amazing my dad was, and I knew they were right. I looked forward to following in his footsteps in my dedication to my church and future family.

My dad and mom made an amazing team. My dad was the provider and the protector, while my mom was the nurturer. Together, they made my growing-up years the dream childhood. With my dad having his hands full with work and church obligations, my mom kept things running smoothly at home.

My mom kept us well fed. There was nothing better than walking in from school and smelling the sweet aroma of freshly baked cookies. Any trauma I might have experienced at school melted away as I devoured those perfectly-melted chocolate chips.

Dinnertime was a daily bonding experience as we gathered around the table eating the meals my mom so diligently cooked for us. She timed it just right, so that after a long day at work, my dad could eat a warm meal before heading off to his evening meetings.

Not only did my mom do all the laundry for our family of eight, she also ironed all of my dad's work and church clothes. To reduce the boredom of long ironing sessions, she would sometimes watch classic black and white movies. I grew to love those old movies and the peace I felt in that small home that was filled with service and love.

My mom's domestic skills were far-reaching. She worked

diligently in her summer garden, producing quite the harvest of vegetables. Not wanting any produce to go to waste, she froze vegetables to enjoy during the winter, and she canned tomatoes to add to future recipes. She also canned salsa, cherries, peaches, pears, and apples. The cherries and peaches were a favorite treat of mine.

My mom also took care of our yard. Without a sprinkler system, she was often busy moving sprinklers around so that our big lawn got plenty of water. To mow the lawn, she used an old-school, non-motorized push lawn mower, which required much strength to push around. I am sure she was excited when some of us got old enough to help with that.

My mom was a skilled seamstress, and she used those skills to save our family money. She fixed and hemmed our clothes that were either ripped or needing altering, bringing life back into clothes that otherwise would have been thrown away. She even made clothing from scratch for us. I was amazed that she even made our prom dresses when needed.

What took her the most time and patience was teaching us how to sew. My sisters were more skilled than I was in this area, but I still remember feeling accomplished when I finished sewing projects with my mom's help. She had to be extremely patient with me. As a bit of a perfectionist, when I made mistakes and had to unpick parts of the project, I got frustrated and wanted to chuck the sewing machine across the room. Somehow, she kept her cool and calmly helped me resolve problems.

Like my dad, my mom was very committed to God and church. She fulfilled her church callings to the best of her ability, and she made sure her children knew the gospel well. I have fond memories of her sharing her testimony with us children in the evenings before bed. I knew the gospel of Jesus Christ meant the world to her as I saw tears roll down her cheeks as she expressed her testimony of gospel principles.

My siblings and I remember one time in particular when my mom displayed that it was a top priority to teach us the gospel. It was not until later in life that we found out that the day we all remember had been an especially long, hard day for my mom. My dad was gone because of a late meeting, and my mom felt like pulling her hair out as she struggled to corral us into bed. When she was finally able to get us settled for the night, she realized she had forgotten to do scripture time with us.

Rather than say, "Oh well," she got creative. She grabbed two bowls from the kitchen and then sat, exhausted, in the hallway next to our bedrooms. She then proceeded to tell the scripture story from the Book of Mormon of how the Jaredites obeyed the Lord by building barges to sail across the ocean to the promised land. She put the bowls together to show how the barges were built to be "tight like . . . a dish" so that water could not get into them while they traveled.[1]

Although we learned that night about the obedience of the Jaredites, what we would always remember was my mom's dedication to the Lord as she listened to the Spirit telling her to teach us that story despite the difficult night.

My parents' actions screamed loudly that they knew the gospel was true, especially their examples of service. What stood out the most to me was the way they served the widows who lived close to us. Lucille lived across the street, and Margaret lived just down the block. My parents were always helping those sweet widows with whatever tasks needed to be done, but I am sure the service those ladies enjoyed the most was the many times my parents would just sit and visit with them.

We children often tagged along on those visits. To be

honest, I remember being bored stiff as the adults had long conversations. I was so bored at Margaret's house that I sat and stared at the unique stitching on the edges of the furniture for what seemed like hours. I analyzed it for so long that I can still remember the curves of the stitches and the buttons that were used as attachments. It was torturous for such a young child to sit that long, but I am glad now that I had the opportunity to see the fruits of service. Watching my parents give up their precious time to care for and visit with those lonely women made me realize what a gift their service was. Those ladies seemed to soak in every minute that we were there.

Margaret needed the most care and attention. My dad went to her house frequently to help with her yard work and fix-it jobs. My mom liked sharing our delicious Sunday dinners with her. My mom would fix up a plate for Margaret, cover it with plastic wrap, and have one or two of the kids deliver it to her on foot, since she lived close by. The kids got a taste of the joy of service as we gave Margaret the plate of food and saw her happiness as she received it.

Eventually, Margaret could no longer care for herself and was moved to the local care facility for the elderly. My parents did not stop taking care of her though. Knowing she did not have family close by, my parents would still go and visit her often.

Towards the end of her life, she got to the point that she was lying in bed most of the time. My parents would find out what she needed or wanted and purchase those items for her. One time Margaret expressed the need for some warmer socks. Not long after, I accompanied my mom on a return visit. My mom sat next to Margaret, who was lying in bed, and proceeded to put new, thick socks on her feet. It was such a tender display of Christlike love.

I also remember my mom bringing Margaret her favorite treat of Fig Newtons. That was such a tender memory because Margaret was so weak at this point that my mom sat with her, ripping off little pieces of those soft cookies and placing them in her mouth for her. Margaret kept saying repeatedly how delicious they were. I will never forget my parents' example of love and kindness.

As you can see, my parents were (and still are) amazing people. It would be easy to grow up with that example and be a little overwhelmed at the prospect of trying to create artwork as beautiful and meaningful as theirs. Fortunately, that was not the case for me. Watching the way my parents lived their lives with joy and dedication gave me a great desire and excitement to emulate their techniques and to create a composition that would have a positive impact on those around me.

As I got older, my greatest desire above all was to follow in my mother's footsteps and to be an amazing wife, mother, and homemaker. I wanted to devote my life to those aspirations. I planned to attend college, get a degree, and get a job as a back-up plan, in case I did not have the opportunity to get married and have kids, but motherhood was my highest priority. My super-motivated self, who as a kid was pushing myself to ride my bike to the top of the hill, was ready to take on all the difficult tasks and challenges of being a mother. I knew through hard work and dedication that I could attain the goal of becoming as amazing as my own mom.

I loved the idea of being an instrumental influence in my children's artistic processes and experiences, helping them create noteworthy masterpieces out of their lives. To raise children from infancy and to mold them into good people did not just sound like a good idea, I knew it was the greatest role that God could place in my hands. After all, as the poem by William Ross Wallace says, "The hand that rocks the cradle is the hand that rules the world."

    I was excited for that prospect, and I felt confident in my abilities to do a good job in the role of wife and mother, especially after having my own mother as such a great example to follow.

5

BLEEDING COLORS

*A*s an artist who learned to color inside the lines to guarantee pleasing results, painting with watercolors frustrated me. Oftentimes with watercolors, a wash technique is used. To do this, you wet the paper with water and apply the colors on top. Because the paper is wet, the colors bleed into each other. Many artists love this technique because of the interesting look the bleeding creates. I, on the other hand, hated not being in total control of the flow of colors. I found it frustrating when the colors would bleed a different direction than I wanted or when the colors pooled in an undesirable spot.

I did not want my life to be like a watercolor. Instead, I wanted to control the exact movement of colors to ensure the desired outcome. It was discouraging when, no matter how hard I tried to control the direction of my life, the colors seemed to bleed in ways I did not want them to.

After two years of college at BYU, I was fortunate to meet the man of my dreams. Tyson was everything I hoped for in a future spouse. He was handsome, kind, considerate, spiritual, a hard worker, and he had a fun personality with a good sense of humor. Although we had our differences, those differences complemented each other, making us a good match. Most importantly, our spiritual goals aligned, and we both wanted more than anything to raise a family together.

I was especially grateful that Tyson was willing to support me in my desire to be a stay-at-home mom. With his mother also being a stay-at-home mom, I think that made the decision an easy one, even though the weight of providing financially for our family would solely be on him. He made my dream of devoting my life to our children a reality, and I will forever feel indebted to him for his sacrifices. I love and appreciate him for the many hours he spent and still spends working his tail off to provide for our family.

Things started off a little tumultuous for us as newlyweds. It was not until later that I realized that I had spent the first six months or so of our marriage depressed, due to the side effects of the birth control I was taking. I thought life was horrible, but it was an illusion. The depression warped my vision of life. There was a lot of crying and sadness on my part during those months, and a lot of confusion and discouragement on Tyson's part. I am sure he wondered what in the world happened to the happy, pleasant girl he thought he married.

Fortunately, I just took birth control long enough that I would still be able to graduate from college before having a baby. Sure enough, as soon as I stopped the birth control, I got pregnant. It was perfect timing because I graduated when I was eight months pregnant. That left me with one month after graduating to prepare for motherhood. That was an exciting time for both of us. With the depression gone and the prospect of welcoming a baby into our lives, we were back to our happy selves.

One month after the birth of our son Jacob, we moved across the country to Kentucky so that Tyson could go to dental school. It was a fun but stressful time as we started a new life in a new place as new parents. We enjoyed our four years in Kentucky, and we made many close friends. Our daughter Sierra was born eighteen months into dental school, so we had our hands extremely full with two kids so close together.

With dental school being so demanding and time consuming for Tyson, I tried to do most of the work associated with taking care of our children and keeping our house clean. Tyson helped as much as time would allow, and he was always willing to step in if I needed him, but school was intense and needed to be his main focus.

My health was not too bad during that time, although I do remember struggling a lot with allergies. Allergies have a way of really sucking the life out of you. It feels like having a mini cold all the time. It just made everyday activities a little bit harder, and I required a lot of naps.

Besides the fatigue and annoyance of the allergies, and the normal difficulties that come with having two young children, I enjoyed our time in Kentucky. I loved all the magical moments of motherhood– taking meandering walks around the neighborhood, going to story time at the library, having play dates with fun friends, tucking the kids in at night and singing songs with them.

Of course, there were times when I felt totally frustrated and overwhelmed because motherhood really is a daily test of patience, but I would not have traded those experiences for the world. I loved my little family, and I felt so grateful to be doing my dream job.

At the end of dental school, Tyson decided to join his dad's dental practice in Boise, Idaho. It was sad to leave Kentucky, but at the same time it was a relief to be done with the rigors of dental school and to live closer to family. We were also excited at the prospect of finally having monthly paychecks come in rather than constantly scrimping by on student loans.

Although we loved most things about Boise, after our move there I seemed to hit an unfavorable turning point with my health. Yes, I had already experienced some discomfort and fatigue from my allergies in Kentucky, but everything seemed to get worse after our move. My allergies started taking over my life, and the exhaustion associated with that really started to hinder my everyday activities. Our son Spencer had been born a few months before moving to Boise, so I thought the fatigue that comes with childbirth would dissipate, but it continued to linger.

Outings with the kids wore me out quickly, and as soon as we would get home, I would crash on the couch. It was so frustrating. I had zero stamina, which made doing anything fun with the children painful. My allergies played a part in wiping me out, but I could tell it was something more. I started needing naps way more than the average person. Something was off in my body. I started turning to doctors to figure out why.

I turned to my OB/GYN first for help. I thought he might be able to help because I could tell that hormones were playing a big part in my gradual decline. I noticed that during certain times of my monthly cycle, my fatigue really kicked in, leaving me physically out of commission.

Unfortunately, he was not much help. He ordered a couple of blood tests that came back normal. Then he told me that if my hormones were off, then the only treatment available was to put my body into artificial menopause through hormone replacement. He did not recommend that as a good option, so he sent me on my way without a good remedy.

One thing the doctor did mention before I left is that it is normal for a mom with three young children to be tired. I am sure he assumed I was overreacting to the normal tiredness all moms feel. I told him that it was more than just the average fatigue, but he brushed it off, and that was the end of that conversation.

I left frustrated. I know he was trying to help, but I felt misunderstood. Maybe I was not emphatic enough about how debilitating the fatigue was, but I was frustrated that he thought that the way I was feeling was normal and just part of motherhood.

The other doctor I went to was an allergy doctor. He had me tested for several outdoor allergies by pricking my back with the most common allergens and then seeing if my skin reacted. When the nurse came back to check for reactions, she let out a gasp.

She said, "Your back is covered in welts! You reacted to almost every allergen!" She measured each welt and recorded the results. She told me with a bit of a laugh, "Well, there were a couple things you did not react to. You're not allergic to molds!"

After learning about my crazy allergies, the doctor recommended allergy shots, which I gladly approved. He told me the shots would reduce, or possibly eliminate, my reactions to those allergens. He told me I would need two shots each time, rather than the one shot that most people get, because of the extreme number of allergies I have. I was so excited to start a treatment that the doctor was optimistic would offer me some relief.

I immediately started the allergy treatments. I do not remember how long it took to notice a difference, but I do remember my allergies improving. My itchy eyes and runny nose went away. Unfortunately, my fatigue did not improve. In fact, it seemed to get worse. Energy became something I just never had enough of. I started to wonder if the allergy shots were causing problems in my body. My fatigue was getting extreme.

You would think that I would simplify my life amid not feeling well, and for the most part I tried to, but for some reason my husband and I got the crazy yearning to add another child to our family. We really wanted to have a big family. Well, as was the norm for us, as soon as we decided to have another baby, we got pregnant.

I have always been full of faith, knowing that God can make all things possible. I figured God would bless me for having the faith to bring another of His special spirits into the world while having health problems. I even thought that maybe showing my faith in that way would bring blessings of improved health and strength. I hoped for a miracle.

The opposite happened; my health immediately declined. Most likely because of the sudden change in my hormonal balance, pregnancy brought major sinus issues. My sinuses became so inflamed that the sinus pressure became unbearable. The inflammation was so extreme that the swollen tissue in my sinuses totally blocked off the passage of air through my nose.

I felt like I was suffocating. I would try to blow my nose to bring some relief, but it was so unproductive because the blockage was mostly just from swollen sinus tissue. Oftentimes it was so bad that when I would try to blow my nose, I could not even get a tiny amount of air through. My nasal airway seemed to be sealed, letting nothing in or out. On top of that, the inflammation in my sinuses created a painful, burning sensation emanating from behind my eyes. The constant pain enveloped me.

It does not seem like inflamed sinuses would be that big of a deal, but it was a nightmare. I felt like my head was in another dimension. I have a vivid memory of trying to have a conversation with a couple of friends and barely being able to get words out.

Have you ever tried plugging your nose and talking? That is kind of what it felt like. I would swallow and my ears and nose would clog up. Then I would try to clear the congestion by blowing air out of my nose, and I would immediately have a total blockage again as soon as I started to talk or swallow.

I was so embarrassed and could not wait for the conversation with my friends to end. My head felt full of snot, yet I could not relieve the pressure in any way. I was so relieved to finally go back home to feel miserable by myself instead of making a fool of myself in front of my friends.

Even sitting on the couch at home was miserable. I remember sitting in the evening, watching television with Tyson, and all I could think about was my stuffy face. I sat there breathing out of my mouth since air would not pass through my nose properly. It was worse than having a cold because blowing my nose did not bring any relief. I felt like I was panting as I sat there, trying to get enough oxygen.

I am sure I drove Tyson crazy, as I could not help but try to constantly clear my airway, even though it was to no avail. Just like when I talked to my friends, my ears and nose would clog up when I swallowed. Then I would try all kinds of things to clear it out. I sat there and sniffed and snorted and cleared my throat to get some sort of passageway for the air to get through. I felt like I was drowning.

It was especially difficult at night when I tried to sleep. I would keep trying to blow my nose repeatedly, and Tyson wondered why I was so inept at nose-blowing. I felt bad for him, as I would lay there and sniff and snort and blow while he was trying to fall asleep.

As bad as the total congestion was, it was not the worst of my symptoms. The overall misery I experienced throughout my body was consuming. Tyson asked me over and over to explain how I felt so he could help me figure out what was wrong, but I could never find the words to help him understand. He wanted so badly to know how to fix my problems.

I was feeling such foreign misery that it did not resemble any illness or pain I had ever experienced before. Therefore, I could not just say, "You know how it feels when . . ." or "It feels just like . . ." I had nothing to compare it to. It was so hard to not have anyone who could completely understand or empathize with my situation because it was such a strange sickness. I wondered if anyone in the world had ever experienced it before. I wanted more than anything to just be able to explain it better to people.

The best explanation I could come up with was an explanation that I heard my friend once use when I asked her about her auto-immune disease. She said, "It kind of feels like I have the flu all the time." That does not perfectly describe how I felt, but it was better than any explanation I could come up with. Like the flu, my body hurt all over. I felt so extremely sick. It seemed that whatever was going on in my sinuses was affecting me everywhere else.

I went to bed most nights feeling at the end of my rope. It was like having the worst cold of my life day after day, knowing I would wake up feeling the same way each morning. Somehow, I held it together most of the time during the daytime, but as the day went on, it would get harder and harder emotionally as the day dragged on. Finally, I could not help but let the despair erupt at bedtime through heavy sobbing.

I remember starting to get ready for bed in our bathroom and just collapsing on the chair by our vanity, crying my eyes out as I sat with my head between my hands. My body hurt so much. My face was miserably congested, the fatigue unbearable. I felt like I could spend the night there crying. Somehow, I got a little relief by just letting all the frustration out through tears. I was quite the sight when I cried because of my swollen sinuses. Crying exacerbated the sniffing and snorting and gasping for air.

I wanted relief, but it seemed nowhere in sight. I wondered if God was aware of my tears. Surely if He saw me sobbing, He must know that this was more than I could bear. I thought that somehow, if I cried hard enough, God would realize that I needed some respite. I cried to lift my white flag in surrender, to tell Heavenly Father I'd had all I could handle. I was desperate for Him to step in and ease my suffering.

Somehow after those long crying sessions of despair, I figured God was ready to step in on my behalf. I would wake up the next day expecting some reprieve. It was disheartening to wake up feeling just as sick as the day before. I was not necessarily crying as a means of showing Heavenly Father I needed Him. I was just so miserable that I had to let out all the negative emotions at the end of the day. I did, however, hope that a by-product of the crying would be God easing my trial.

After three months of the horrible congestion, body pain, and fatigue, things finally improved. That is when it became clear that the debilitating symptoms were a phenomenon related to the hormones of the first trimester of pregnancy. I was so thankful to be out of that dark phase. Things were not perfect after that, but I felt like I had a new lease on life with the symptoms no longer taking over my existence.

The next phase of my health issues did not come into play until I gave birth that June. Everything started to unravel right there in the hospital room after having Malea. In the middle of the night, as I lay in the hospital bed recovering from childbirth, all of the sudden I started to struggle to breathe.

I tried to focus on breathing, slowing down each inhalation and exhalation so I could hopefully get my breathing under control. That did not seem to help. In fact, it got worse. I started gasping for air, and quickly realized I needed some help. I pushed the button to alert the nurse that I needed her, and I started to panic as I waited for her to come.

I explained to her what was going on, and thankfully she was quick to respond as she ran off to get backup. She returned quickly with helpers to give me a breathing treatment of albuterol. As I breathed that medicine in, I felt my body and my lungs immediately relax. It felt so amazing to just be able to breathe normally again. My shallow, fast breaths turned into slow, methodical ones, and I immediately drifted off to sleep as my body found reprieve from the panic of that night's episode.

It felt like everything started to go wrong after that. At one point during my hospital stay, I noticed a strange rash on the side of my hip. Although it was a small area, it was itchy, thick, and bumpy. I pointed out the area of concern to the doctor. To my surprise, he told me it was Shingles. I had heard of it but did not know much about it. The doctor explained to me that Shingles is a reactivation of the chickenpox virus in the body, causing a painful rash.

I have since learned that Shingles can be awfully miserable for a lot of people. Fortunately for me, I had a mild case. It did not bother me much; it was just an annoyance, but it was one more red flag that showed my immune system was crashing.

To add to the mix, Malea ended up catching chickenpox from me. Little did I know that Shingles would make me contagious with the chickenpox virus. It was a strange dynamic, because not only did I give her chickenpox, but I also gave her some immunity to it by nursing her with mother's milk, making it a very mild case. It is rare for small babies to get chickenpox, but when they do it is often fatal. It was perplexing that I gave Malea chickenpox but also gave her immunity to it at the same time.

When I got home from the hospital, my body kept having issues. The asthma attack I had experienced in the hospital was the beginning of a new asthmatic condition for me. The new asthma was totally different than what I had experienced in high school. The exercise-induced asthma I had in high school only affected me when I played competitive sports, when I pushed my body to the limit physically. Since I had not played competitive sports in several years, I no longer had an issue with that kind of asthma. In fact, I had not had an asthma attack since high school, so I had forgotten I was even asthmatic, up until that traumatic episode in the hospital.

After I got home from the hospital, I started having asthma attacks every day. It was strange to go from only being asthmatic if I ran, to having an asthma attack at random times when I was just sitting around feeding the baby or lying down at night to go to sleep. It did not make sense. I could not correlate the asthma attacks to anything I was doing.

Luckily, they sent me home from the hospital with an inhaler, because I started puffing on that thing several times a day to keep my lungs functioning. Gasping for air became part of my daily routine, followed quickly by a dose of Albuterol.

The next stage of my health collapse was a strange rash all over the trunk of my body. This was totally different from the Shingles rash I had gotten in the hospital. This new rash looked like little, red halos sporadically covering mostly my stomach and back. It was a little itchy but did not bother me much otherwise. I was hopeful that the rash would be an obvious sign that would help the doctor recognize and diagnose what was going wrong in the rest of my body.

Unfortunately, the rash just added to the mystery of my bad health. I went to the doctor, and I could tell by the expression on his face that he had no idea what that rash was. He then told me, with hesitation in his voice, that the rash was probably caused by a virus and that time would most likely be the remedy. I went on my way, a little bummed that the rash was not the magic puzzle piece that would make everything else make sense. On the bright side, at least the rash did end up resolving on its own.

Although the rashes and constant asthma attacks were not fun, the worst part of my health decline was the severe fatigue. I realized that the lack of sleep that comes with a newborn was part of the problem, but the fatigue was worse than anything I had ever experienced with my other three children's births.

When I went to my follow-up appointment with my OB/GYN, I mentioned my overall decline in energy. He did not seem concerned, which was annoying. He had heard me talk about my lack of energy before, so it was not a surprise to him. It was so hard to function, and I really wanted something to help. He did some blood testing like he had done a couple years earlier, to check for any major health issues, and somehow it did not make me feel better when I came back to hear the results, only to have him tell me, "You are actually very healthy."

I felt like screaming back, "No I am NOT!!" How could I be healthy if I felt so sick?!?

Life became miserable. Do not get me wrong; I had many, many things to be grateful for, including supportive family and friends. We were also blessed with financial security and everything we needed monetarily, but I was miserable despite my gratitude for all those things. The body pain, sinus pain, and fatigue were so difficult to push through. Each daily task associated with motherhood felt like a huge mountain to climb. Laundry, dishes, cooking, and chauffeuring children around became monumental tasks to overcome each day. Each time one of the children would need help with something, it felt like they were asking me to climb Mt. Everest.

There must have been enough fairly good days mixed in with the bad, because it was not long before I got the yearning to have another baby. I think it was a divinely driven desire because it really did not make any sense to add another baby to our family at that time. I was struggling to take care of the children we already had.

After only a month or so of trying to get pregnant, I came to my senses and realized I was in no condition to bring another child into the world. I remember the day I decided it was not a good idea to get pregnant.

Tyson wanted to take the kids to do something fun on a Saturday. I stayed home with Malea since I was not feeling well and since she was too young for the activity. I felt extremely sick, although I knew it was just my normal fatigue and pain, not a virus. My suffering was so intense that I spent the day sitting on the couch trying to cope. Eventually I could not take it anymore, and the tears just started rolling down my face. The pain seemed unbearable. I was at the end of my rope emotionally. I felt so alone.

What I remember most about that day was my toddler's reaction. Malea curled up next to me on the couch when she saw me crying. Concern and tenderness filled her eyes, and she instinctively reached up and started gently wiping the tears off my face with her pudgy fingers. Her simple, sweet act of compassion lightened my load. She was my angel that day, comforting me when no one else could.

It hit me that it would not be smart to get pregnant when I felt so unhealthy. The fatigue and pain were too debilitating. That night, I told Tyson we needed to change our plans, and he totally understood and agreed.

Well, Heavenly Father had His own plan in mind for us. We did stop trying to get pregnant, but miraculously we still got pregnant. Once again, I was full of faith and thought surely Heavenly Father would heal me of my health problems so I could deal with being pregnant, along with taking care of our other four children.

Once again, my pregnancy started out with horrible inflammation in my sinuses. I could not breathe out of my nose, and I was totally miserable. As bad as it was, I reassured myself that it would most likely be like my previous pregnancy, where the suffering only lasted for the first trimester. I waited and waited for the symptoms to calm down, but they never did. Finally realizing that this time it was not just a first trimester problem, I went to my doctor hoping to find something, anything to help relieve my sinus pain.

It is especially difficult to have health problems during

pregnancy because all of the sudden it becomes much riskier to take any kind of medication. I tried so hard not to take anything because I did not want to cause any issues with the baby, but eventually I got desperate.

I honestly got to the point where I wished I did not have to live anymore, so I figured it would be better to try medication than to feel that hopeless. My doctor recommended I try using a nasal spray medication for my sinuses. It was a class C medication, meaning animal studies have "shown an adverse effect on the fetus and there are no adequate and well-controlled studies in humans, but potential benefits may warrant use of the drug in pregnant women despite potential risks."[1]

It sounded risky, but I hesitantly started using the nasal spray anyway. My doctor reassured me, saying that with a nasal spray, the medication is so localized in the sinuses that there would not be much absorbed into the bloodstream. Since he did not seem concerned, I felt better taking it. Of course, as a worried mother, I still had concerns and was prayerful that the baby would be healthy.

I started using the nasal spray religiously but never noticed a difference. I started doing sinus rinses, but they did not seem to help either. In addition, I resorted to taking decongestants, which also did not bring relief.

That pregnancy was by far the hardest nine months of my life. It is hard to explain misery in words. In fact, I dread trying to explain my illness in writing for fear of being misunderstood. For the most part, there really are no words to explain how horrible I felt.

To this day, I am amazed that God required such extreme suffering on my part. I wonder how an all-loving Father in Heaven could watch one of His daughters suffer so long and so much. I am still brought to tears when I think about those days. It truly felt like more than I could bear.

My life had become a watercolor wash, with colors bleeding in directions I could not control or handle. The colors pooled and looked muddy.

This was not the design I had planned out.

6

HIDDEN LAYERS

This might sound strange, but I feel such empathy for my former self, the young mother who was in constant pain and always suffering. That young mother was living righteously in hopes of gaining the blessings of heaven. That young mother wanted nothing more than to feel well enough to take care of her husband and children, and to please her Father in Heaven. It pains me to think of the many tears that drenched my pillow night after night as I wondered how I could possibly endure another day of pain and sickness. It truly seemed more than I could bear, and no amount of crying or pleading with my Heavenly Father improved the situation.

There was one point where Tyson and I decided to ask our home teacher to come help Tyson give me a priesthood blessing. I was full of so much faith, hoping that a blessing of health would put me on the road to recovery and relief. I knew that God could heal me with a priesthood blessing.

Our home teacher came to our house, and I think we were all surprised at the words of the blessing. Rather than being told that I would experience a miracle of improved health, I was told that the suffering I was experiencing was part of my earthly experience that I would endure. As the blessing ended, our friend looked at us both and said something like, "Well, that was interesting. I'm sure that was not what you were hoping to hear."

We all kind of laughed a little at the situation and the unexpected blessing. Although it was a little comical, I was beyond disappointed. At the same time, the blessing did bring me peace that God knew me and knew I was suffering. I was not alone.

I also concluded, as I thought of the vast amount of suffering I was enduring, that Heavenly Father must have really thought it was important for me to experience those things or He would have relieved me of those horrific experiences. Like a loving earthly father, my Heavenly Father would not want me, His child, to endure any suffering that is not for my ultimate benefit, learning, and experience.

Despite not getting a blessing of healing that day, I was blessed with the realization that He is aware of me and wants what is best for me. Knowing I was in my Heavenly Father's constant watchful care brought me peace in my suffering. I just needed to take one day at a time with the challenges I was facing.

Those torturous nine months ended with the birth of a perfect baby girl. The immediate hour after Kayla was born was unlike anything I had ever experienced. It was as if the doors of heaven were opened. That tiny baby acted as if she understood the gravity of her birth and what it took to get her there. I tried to feed her, but she had no desire. She just lay there in my arms in total peace and contentment.

I will never forget her lying there so peacefully, looking around the room for so long. It was as if my precious baby could see angels around that hospital room, heralding her birth. Her eyes did not have the expected oblivious look that one would expect from a baby who knows nothing of the world she just entered. There was such a feeling of understanding and reverence in her countenance.

Somehow, life's good moments become so much sweeter when they are intertwined with hardship. The birth of Kayla was truly magnificent.

Then my suffering resumed. I have to say that nothing after that pregnancy would ever quite compare to the overall extremity of pain and discomfort I experienced, but my suffering did continue, and I wondered if I would ever feel well again.

I hoped that once the pregnancy ended that my health would return. As I mentioned, the severity of the symptoms did subside to a point, but my life was never the same after that. My life continued to be devoid of energy, and I felt sick every day. Some days were worse than others, but each day contained a certain amount of suffering.

My sinuses did not recover. Although they were not totally blocked off like they were when I was pregnant, there was enough inflammation that they always made me feel congested and in pain. It often felt like a burning sensation behind my eyes. It was difficult to have so much pain in my head and face. Having the discomfort in that location made it impossible to ignore. It took center stage. Sometimes I wished the pain were in a different part of my body, farther away from my head. It was hard to think, and it was challenging to avert my focus away from the misery.

Sinus infections became a way of life. Since my sinuses were so clogged, they were a perfect breeding ground for infections. Every time I caught a cold, my sinuses would get infected. I would try to wait it out to see if they would heal on their own, but they never did. I would wait until I could not take it anymore, and then I would go to the doctor to be prescribed antibiotics.

I knew antibiotics were not good for me to take repeatedly, but there seemed to be no other solution. I dreaded taking them because my body always reacted badly. Taking them made me feel worse instead of better, so I would take them long enough to get rid of the infections and then I would be relieved when I got to stop taking them. Sometimes I would not take them the prescribed number of days because of how sick they made me feel. I would hesitantly stop taking them and hope that my body would still recuperate.

This cycle was difficult: I would have cold symptoms for a week; it would turn into a sinus infection; I would give my body a week or two of time to heal on its own (which it never seemed to do); and then I would take antibiotics for ten days. By the time I finally recovered from what should have been a little cold, I would catch another cold and the cycle would start all over again. Whenever our children came home from school with a cold, I wanted to cry because I knew I was a goner. My immune system was never strong enough to avoid catching it from them. I knew it would be a month of misery to follow.

I wish I had kept a better journal of my life during those years, but I just could not. With my sinuses hurting most of the time, anything that took focus or thought seemed impossible, including writing or reading. I spent so much time on the couch, and I felt like I was wasting my life away. You would think that would be the perfect opportunity to do something semi-productive, like writing in my journal, but it was just too painful. My head was in a fog, and even lying on the couch was extremely uncomfortable and difficult.

I do have some memories that I can recall from those hard times. One memory I have is trying to drive our children around to their various activities. With five children, as much as I tried to keep activities to a minimum, there were always a lot of things going on. To be honest, some of the driving I brought on myself because I really wanted our children to take music lessons and to have opportunities to play sports.

It seems like driving should be a relaxing, easy thing to do, even for someone not feeling great, but it was oftentimes miserable and even unbearable at times. I have vivid memories of being in the car, taking a child somewhere they needed to be, and just wanting to cry. I wanted so badly to lie down. I hurt all over. Just sitting there in the car was so painful. I felt so sick, especially in my sinuses, making it so difficult to sit there. I remember dropping off children at activities and then crying as I drove home because I hated the way my body felt.

I have another memory that happened sometimes as I was driving kids around. Sometimes I would be at a stoplight or waiting in traffic, and I would have the distinct thought, *All these people around me have no idea how badly I am hurting.* Similarly, I had the thought that I had no idea what the people in the cars next to me might be going through. I wondered if drivers would be much more considerate and understanding of other drivers on the road if they knew the burdens that each person is bearing.

Everyone bustles around, sometimes getting angry with a driving mistake that the driver next to them makes. I think we would always treat each other with more compassion and empathy if we all wore our trials written on our foreheads. One time I was in the Walmart parking lot, and someone got mad at me for taking the parking spot she wanted. She made it very clear that she was mad by shaking her finger at me and mouthing angry words. It made me feel horrible.

It was a total accident on my part. Since I had not seen her car coming around the corner, I was totally oblivious that she wanted that spot. I would not have taken that spot if I had known she thought she had dibs on it.

I wondered if she would have treated me differently if she knew the amount of pain I was experiencing. Because I felt so miserable, it took every ounce of energy I had to drag myself in and out of the store. A closer parking spot made a big difference in my day, with exhaustion making it painful to even walk a little farther away. I also felt that I needed to try to see things from her perspective. Maybe she was easily angered because of huge trials in her own life. Maybe she had layers to her painting that I could not see.

Years ago, I saw a short video called "Glasses of Empathy" that made a big impact on me. It showed a man going about his day and being annoyed by all the people he encountered. He was irritated by a neighborhood boy who got in his way as he backed out of his driveway, by a lady who took his parking spot, by a man who cut in front of him in line at a coffee shop, by a worker who was slow getting him his coffee, etc. When he sat down to wait for his coffee, a mysterious man walked up, handed him an eye-glasses case that said *Get Service*, and disappeared.

After putting on the glasses from the case, whenever he looked at someone, he magically saw what trial they were going through. For example, written next to people whom he was originally irritated with, were things like *Recently lost his job, Fighting addiction,* and *Grieving her best friend*. Then when he went home, he saw, written next to the neighborhood boy, *Just needs someone to care*. The man decided to change his attitude and his actions. The video ends with the man befriending the boy and trying to uplift him and make him feel special.[1]

That video was eye-opening and helped me to look at people differently. It helped me realize that everyone has hidden challenges, and everyone would benefit from increased kindness, understanding, and love. The world would be a much better place if we would give each other the benefit of the doubt and not pass judgment on each other.

Many art pieces contain hidden layers that are not noticeable. Especially with oil paintings, I end up adding several layers before producing the desired effect. Looking at the finished product, you would not know how much went into the creation. Sometimes it takes layers of difficulty and mistakes before getting the piece to where I want it to be.

In the same way, looking at me, you would not know I had hidden layers of intense suffering. The pain was not obvious from the outside. I looked healthy. I would sit in church, wanting so badly to lie down on the bench because I felt extremely sick and in pain. Even holding the hymn book felt like a chore with my limited energy.

I imagined people around us probably looked at our young family, with our cute children lined up on the bench, thinking we had it so easy. They might have thought that it was not fair that we had a life devoid of trials, when in actuality, I could barely stand to be alive at times.

I was so fortunate to be able to make it to church with how sick I felt. That was one of the miracles I experienced during those years of sickness. I truly believe that God had a hand in helping me get our young family to church each week. Tyson had to be at the church early for meetings because of his church callings, so I was left to get our family ready by myself.

I believe it was not by chance that I felt well enough each

Sunday morning to get our five kids ready for church. It was no small feat, as any young mother could attest. I imagine there were angels around me, bearing me up, helping me get my family fed, dressed and out the door for church. It was so easy at times to feel like the Lord was not hearing my prayers during my health trials, but looking back, I now see that He helped me accomplish the most critical things. I got my family to the chapel each week to partake of the sacrament. No other family activity was more important than that. It truly was a miracle.

Grocery shopping, as pathetic as it sounds, was one of my biggest challenges each week. I felt like I dragged sandbags around with me as I pushed the shopping cart around. Each aspect of grocery shopping drained my already depleted energy supply. By the time I got home and had to transport groceries from my car to the house, I felt ready to collapse. I would painfully put away anything that needed to be kept in the refrigerator or freezer, and then leave the rest to be put away another time, as I collapsed on the couch or my bed to sleep.

One time, I was already out and about doing another errand when I needed to stop at the grocery store. I was already at a point of total exhaustion, but since I was right by the store, I pulled into the parking lot. I needed a nap so desperately, and I realized I did not have enough energy to walk into the store. I sat and debated on what to do. It seemed ridiculous to drive all the way home, take a nap, and then drive all the way back to the store, but I wanted to cry when I thought about the alternative of trying to walk into the grocery store right then.

I made what seemed like a crazy decision. I decided to take a nap in my car right there in the parking lot. I hoped to afterward wake up with enough energy to go into the store.

Luckily, the weather was perfect for this plan, not too hot or too cold to be in the car for an hour. I locked my car doors for safety, climbed back into the very back row of our minivan, and laid down to take a nap. I hoped that with the van's heavily tinted windows, nobody in the parking lot would look into the back windows and see me, a grown woman, taking a nap in my minivan. They would surely think I was either crazy or dead.

The plan ended up working perfectly. I got the much-needed sleep, and I woke up with enough energy to carry out the task ahead of me. I was so grateful to be able to get the job done without going home first to take a nap. At the same time, it was so sad that such a menial task was such a monumental event for me, and that it was so difficult to accomplish. Life in general just felt extremely hard.

As much as I truly loved being a mother and felt so grateful to have five amazing children, my disease made it so painful to take care of them. One time I was lying on the couch feeling horrible when Spencer walked in from outside with his boots on. Before I realized it, he had walked all the way across the living room and down the hall, leaving mud prints on the wood floor and carpet with each step. Knowing he did not do it on purpose and was too young to realize the damage he had done, I held my tongue, even though I felt like screaming out of frustration.

I knew it would be way more difficult to remove the mud if I left it to dry, so I peeled myself off the couch to clean up the mess. It took every ounce of strength I had. I got a wet, soapy rag and got down on my hands and knees and started to scrub. Tears rolled down my face, miserable and exhausted as I followed the tracks, crawling and scrubbing. I felt horrible. I hated that such a small mistake by my sweet child became an act of torture for me to clean up. Scrubbing a little dirt off the carpet should have been a simple task, yet I felt like a sick runner trying to finish the last mile of a marathon.

Mornings were especially difficult, as I would wake up with my sinuses killing me. It did not help that I usually woke up after a horrible night of tossing and turning, being unable to sleep well. One morning, I dragged myself to join our children at the table for our daily breakfast of cold cereal since I did not have energy to cook anything for them. As I walked up to the table, somehow I knocked the box of Cheerios over, and cereal flew all over the floor.

I was feeling so incredibly horrible that I knew if I tried to clean up the cereal at that moment that I would either scream or cry or both, so I chose what I thought was the higher road and did not clean it up at all. I grabbed my bowl of cereal and sat down and started to eat, trying to ignore the mess and to control my emotions that felt at a tipping point.

To my surprise, Jacob jumped up from his seat, grabbed the broom from the pantry and started sweeping up my mess. I was totally surprised and grateful. He did it so instinctively that I wondered if the Spirit whispered to him to do what I could not do at that moment.

I was so grateful for the hundreds of times our children stepped in to do the things I felt that I could not. At the same time, I was filled with remorse for not being able to truly mother them the way I had always envisioned. It felt wrong for such small children to have to take care of their mom. I wanted to take care of them.

7

DOUBTING THE PROCESS

When I first became a mother and my disease had not kicked in yet, I was able to delve into the artistic process with ease. I was confident in my ability to create the desired outcome of my life as well as the lives of our children. I shared so many special moments with our young children.

Since Jacob was the oldest, he got the best version of me as far as energy and attention goes. We shared many tender moments together. Our nighttime routine was especially bonding. I would go with him to his room, kneel with him as he said his nightly prayer, and then tuck him into bed and sing him songs. Then I would leave him with a hug and a kiss.

It was such a disappointment to not have those same moments with all our children.

I remember lying on the couch, crying in total misery when it was time to get the children in bed. I could not tuck them in bed, sing to them, or help them say their prayers. I felt so guilty to send them off to bed by just saying, "Go to bed, please."

Most nights we did have family prayer together before bed, but I worried that they would not learn to say their individual prayers without me by their side, encouraging them each night like my mom did.

With Jacob, I had many fun adventures with him when he was little. I loved going on walks around the neighborhood as he would discover the wonderful world of nature. I loved taking him to local parks to play and get his energy out. We also had fun going to the library for story time and songs. I planned play dates with friends, and we joined a preschool co-op where the mothers took turns teaching each school day.

I felt so much guilt when I could not do the same thing with our other children. I remember driving past our neighborhood park, and one of the children would see other neighborhood kids out playing and ask if we could go to the park. I had to hold back the tears as I knew that going to the park was more than I could handle. Even sitting on a bench to watch them play was too much for me. Time after time, I would sadly tell my kids that we could not go to the park, and it made me so sad.

There were times when I was able to make the trek to the park, but those times were rare, so I felt like our children were missing out on an important part of childhood. I began to doubt the artistic process when I could not control the medium anymore. How could I create the desired results without a healthy body?

When Kayla was three, she attended preschool a few days a week in the mornings, and I was so grateful for that. I used the time that she was there to try to get the necessities done like shopping or laundry. After I picked her up, I had no energy left, so I would lie in my bed with her and read her a couple of books until I fell asleep. As I drifted off to sleep, I could feel her giving me one kiss after another. Sometimes she would play with my hand and intertwine her fingers with mine. Other times she would wrap her cute, chubby arms around me and fall asleep with me.

There were days that Kayla was not tired, and I could feel her bouncing around on my bed, trying to entertain herself. It was so sad to me that, rather than doing crafts or something fun with her mom, she was there entertaining herself next to her sleeping mom each day.

There were also times when I would fall asleep on the couch, and I would hear Kayla talking to herself as I drifted in and out of sleep. When I woke up, I would find funny videos on our iPad because, while I was sleeping, she would lie on her stomach on the floor, propped up with her arms, and she would record herself saying random things as she looked at herself in the iPad. It was funny but kind of sad that she had nothing better to do because I spent so much time sleeping.

I also remember Malea needing to take care of herself from a young age. When she was around four, I remember being sick on the couch when she wanted to eat some lunch. I would give her step-by-step directions on how to make something simple for herself. I remember instructing her, "Okay, open the fridge, grab the package of hot dogs that should be right in front of you on the middle shelf. Close the fridge. Get a plate out of the bottom drawer. Take a hot dog out and put it on the plate. Push a chair in front of the microwave. Stand on the chair and put the plate in the microwave. Close the microwave. Push the number two. Then push the number zero. Then push start."

At first, I would have to help her figure out which buttons

were the right ones to push. She would hold her finger over a button while I instructed her to move her finger up, down, or over to get to the correct button. Eventually she did not need my help. I felt so bad that I could not just get up and make her something.

I hated that I could not serve my family the way I had always hoped. I felt like our children were deprived of the kind of amazing mother I had. It worried me that they would not have a good example to look to for how a mother should be. How could they produce worthwhile artwork without a positive artistic influence to look to for inspiration? I worried they would think all mothers are lazy and just lie on the couch and ask for help with everything.

Out of desperation, there were so many little tasks that I had to ask the children to help me with. I remember not having the energy to give Kayla baths when she was a toddler. I waited until she was in desperate need, and then I would ask Jacob or Sierra to give her one. It was stressful for me as I gave them step-by-step instructions on how to do it safely. Then when things did not go perfectly and they needed back-up, I would send in one of the other children to help them grab a towel or whatever was needed. Although I felt bad that I had to give such young children my adult responsibilities, it also brought me such relief when they brought out Kayla nice and clean after she needed a bath so badly.

Another thing our children had to help me with frequently was the cleaning. I felt guilty that Tyson would often come home to a house that was a disaster at the end of the day, so I would often put the children to work cleaning up. I remember lying on the couch when they got home from school, and I would make the announcement that I needed everyone to help clean for a half hour before they could do anything else.

I became the director. They were too young at the time to just tell them to clean, and it would happen. Instead, I would have to continually say things like, "Spencer, grab those shoes over here. Go put them in your closet." "Sierra, get a rag wet and wipe off the table. Make sure to put the garbage can by the table so you can wipe the crumbs into it." "Malea, grab the books that are scattered on the floor and put them on the bookshelf in the office." "Jacob, get the vacuum and vacuum this area. No, do not put the vacuum away yet, you missed this spot over here." "Kayla, get the silverware holder out of the dishwasher; put it on the counter; stand on a chair next to the silverware drawer and put the silverware in the drawer." It amazed me at the difference it made to our home when all those little hands worked together to clean up.

One of the hardest parts of my health trial was the guilt. I felt like I was failing at life. I always wondered if I was not trying hard enough, if I was not pushing through the pain enough, and if I just was not enough. There were days when I persevered better than others, which made me feel even more guilt on the bad days. Why could I not push through every day?

I wondered why I was so weak. More than anything, I hated feeling lazy and unproductive. Lying on the couch and getting nothing done was so difficult. I questioned if I was in good standing with the Lord. Was He pleased with my performance as I lay useless on the couch? It was hard to imagine that He possibly could be. I needed to mark off a checklist to feel valuable, and nothing was checked off.

In a way, sometimes it felt like a relief when I got sick with a flu or cold because then I felt less guilt when I spent the day on the couch. I liked giving myself the excuse that I had a "real" sickness and that my body needed rest to recuperate. With my chronic illness, knowing it was not going away any time soon, the guilt was always there. I constantly questioned if I was pushing hard enough to be productive. Resting one day did not result in feeling rested and recuperated the next day. Resting just left me more behind on things I needed to get done eventually.

Dinner was my nemesis and often the center of my guilt. My family needed me to provide that. With our children being so young, they could help prepare simple lunch items, but dinner was not something I could tell them to cook for themselves. I am sure they would have survived off grilled cheese and cold cereal, but it did not seem fair to force Tyson to eat that every night.

After seeing my mom be so successful at having dinner on the table promptly each night so my dad could be satiated after a long day at work, I felt horrible not doing the same for Tyson. I wanted so intensely to do that for him. He deserved it. He worked so hard at a stressful job he did not enjoy; the least I could do was feed him dinner when he got home. As the homemaker, that should be one of my main responsibilities.

Dinnertime was the hardest part of the day. I could often get things done early in the day, but as the day drew on, I felt worse and worse. By the time dinnertime rolled around, I was miserable. Sometimes I managed to drag myself around the kitchen to put together a meal, wanting more than anything to lie down. Other times I called Tyson on the way home from work to pick up fast food.

Too often, Tyson would walk in, exhausted from work, and I would be asleep on the couch with the children running around, and no meal in sight. It must have been frustrating and disappointing for him when he was starving and ready to crash for the day. He was always kind and loving about it, but I know it was difficult for him to have a dysfunctional wife.

I concluded that I must be his greatest trial, and I hated that. I wanted to make his life easier, not harder. It must have been so difficult to be married to me. I'm sure he assumed our marriage would be one of equal partnership, but I was not much of an equal partner with how often he had to pick up my slack. I knew it was important to serve my spouse to show my love, but I did not know how to do that without any energy.

The pain and misery were so invisible to others that I felt crazy. Surely my sickness could not just be in my mind, but it was hard when I assumed others thought it was. I had a few people talk to me about depression, hoping to help me find a solution to get my stamina back, but I knew I was not depressed. I understood why they thought it could be depression since the symptoms are similar, and I appreciated that they cared about me enough to try to help, but I felt misunderstood. To me it was the opposite of depression because I had a deep desire and drive to do the things I loved; but, unlike depression, it was my body rather than my mind that was not cooperating.

I did try antidepressants at one point since so many people thought they would help. I was willing to try anything that might improve my symptoms. Taking antidepressants ended up creating an adverse effect; they made me depressed. When I immediately started having suicidal thoughts, I knew I had to stop taking them.

Although that experiment failed, it was beneficial to experience what real depression felt like so I could cross that off my list of possible culprits. I think people around me thought I must be embarrassed or in denial about having depression; but, if anything, I applaud those with depression for facing such extreme difficulty. I did get sad and discouraged frequently, but that is a normal reaction to being sick and in pain every day. I knew my sickness could lead to depression eventually, but so far, I was fine in that regard.

Although I was glad I did not have depression, it was frustrating that I was not able to get a diagnosis. If I had found out it was depression, at least I would know what was wrong with me, and I would have medication options that would improve my circumstances.

I felt like I was given the exact art medium that I did not want and could not handle. I could have made something beautiful with oil paints, so why was I given watercolors?

When I was younger, I thought about some of the trials I could face with ease. For example, I always thought I would be poor when I grew up and that I would handle it well. I felt like I would be good at that trial. I knew how to do without, and I did not need anything extravagant or fancy to be happy. I knew how to be resourceful and frugal. For some reason, I thought that would be the test I would be given and that I would pass with flying colors. Maybe it would not have been easy for me, but I thought it would be. You can imagine my surprise when I got engaged to Tyson, who declared he was going to be a dentist! Wait, what!?! I'm supposed to be poor!

I assumed I would have trials that would be manageable. Since I am a hard worker and an overachiever, I figured I could push myself through any challenge. Instead, I faced trials that other people might have found easy but for me caused extreme heartache and discouragement. My challenges seemed tailor-made to be unbearable for me.

I wanted so badly to work hard and achieve great things, and that is exactly what I could not do. Being forced to be idle, I felt like my worth as a person decreased. I could not figure out why the Lord would not make it possible for me to do worthwhile things with my life. I felt like I had so much potential and that I spent my days on the couch squandering it. Why was the Lord not fixing my problems so I could get on with my life?

I wanted so badly to be a fun, active mom. I envisioned myself using my energy and athleticism to play sports with our children and to spend time doing fun activities with them. I wanted to be as industrious as my mom was. I wanted to clean, cook, garden, can, and sew, and I wanted to teach my kids how to do all those things. I wanted to take my kids to the park and the library. I wanted to develop and expand my talents in music and art. I wanted to serve my neighbors and uplift those around me. I wanted to magnify my church callings and to be a blessing to those I served.

Those were all worthwhile aspirations that Heavenly Father should want me to fulfill. He should heal me so I could become who I had the potential to be. I could be a magnificent instrument in His hands, creating exquisite artwork, if given the means.

Shouldn't He want that for me?

8

DESIGN ADJUSTMENTS

My search for answers to my health issues ensued. If there was a cure out there, I was determined to find it. I prayed with faith that God would help me find those answers. I knew that God, who is all-knowing, could lead me to the artistic adjustments that would improve the aesthetics of my design.

As I sought ways to improve my health, I often got advice from people in my life. One friend suggested I try going to her naturopathic doctor. I loved the idea of finding more natural means to treat my sickness. That sounded much better than taking medications that have a whole slew of side effects.

The naturopath had me do a blood test to see if I had any food allergies. When the results came back, I was so excited! The test showed I was allergic to dairy, wheat, gluten, and peanuts. The naturopath gave me advice on how to avoid those foods and how to replace them with other food options. She gave me hope that drastically changing my diet would bring relief from my sinus pain and body fatigue. I was SO excited!

You would not think that taking everything delicious out of my life would be exciting, but I was ecstatic to have answers and to finally have control of the situation. It seemed like a small price to pay to get relief from years of sickness.

My hope soared, thinking I had discovered the remedy for my problems. I left the appointment walking on air, and I went right to work figuring out a diet and menu plan to follow. It was not easy by any means to change my diet so extensively, but it was worth it. I immediately started feeling better, and I was thrilled. My energy levels increased, and my sinuses felt better. I was ready to shout from the rooftops that I was cured! It felt amazing to get my life back.

Fortunately, I delayed my shout from the rooftops. The improvement in my health did not last long. I kept up with the diet so strictly. I was not going to let food get in the way of me feeling better; but, despite my dedication, my bad health gradually returned to square one. I could not figure out why the diet was not working anymore. I started altering the diet in various ways, thinking I was just not doing it correctly. None of the alterations made a difference, or at least not a big enough difference to notice.

After months of trial and error, I decided it was not worth struggling through the diet anymore. I was willing to put in the work and to give up any food, but not if it was not helping. I do not know why the diet worked for a while and then stopped. Was it only a placebo effect?

I have no idea, but it was heartbreaking. I got a little taste of a return to normalcy, and it was devastating to feel sick once again. I ended up telling my allergy doctor about the naturopath appointment and allergy test, and he told me, in a matter of words, that the allergy test I took was a crock. It was not a legitimate test for discovering food allergies.

Although I was sad the diet did not solve my problems, it was a bit of a relief to start eating normally again. I always wondered after that, though, why the diet helped for a short duration, and if food somehow played a part in my health decline. I could tell that I often felt worse after eating, but I could not pinpoint which foods made that happen. It seemed random. I had to set those worries aside for a while; it was mentally exhausting to constantly question the effect of every food I ate.

Over a year later, I came across another possible remedy. I noticed that every night when I went to bed, my asthma kicked in and I had to use my rescue inhaler. I could not figure out why nighttime was a trigger. It did not make sense. Then one day we were out and about when one of the children handed me a piece of gum. I am not much of a gum chewer, but I accepted it. Not long after starting to chew it, I felt my lungs tighten up, and my breathing became labored. It was not a severe asthma attack, but it was bad enough that I had to use my rescue inhaler.

That was the missing puzzle piece I needed. It helped me realize that the common denominator in my nighttime routine and the gum-chewing incident was mint. I used mint toothpaste every night before bed, and the gum I chewed was mint flavored. It was an easy fix to take mint out of my life.

I immediately replaced my toothpaste with a berry flavored one, which I did not enjoy, but it made my nightly asthma attacks end. It was not a life-altering change, however. Most of my symptoms were still an issue, but it did initiate another discovery. I did some research online and found that mint is a salicylate. Salicylates are natural chemicals found in fruits and vegetables that help protect plants against disease and insects.

Delving into the subject more, I discovered a low-salicylate diet benefited some people with respiratory issues. Maybe this was the cure I had been praying for.

Once again, I jumped in with both feet, ready to commit fully to a diet that might offer some relief. The diet entailed getting rid of some of the healthiest food options, which seemed counterintuitive. The level of salicylates is highest in the most colorful fruits and vegetables, which are also the healthiest ones. It is impossible to eliminate all salicylates from a diet, but the goal with the low-salicylate diet was to keep the amount of salicylates at a minimum.

The positive effect of the diet was immediate. I could not believe it! I felt like a new person. All of the sudden, my body started to function well, and it was miraculous. It was amazing to have my health return so quickly and so completely.

The first positive moments are ingrained in my memory. I went to the grocery store one of those first days, and it felt like the best day of my life. It made me realize just how difficult my life had really been because of my bad health. I distinctly remember walking from my car and into the store with no pain. A huge weight was lifted off my shoulders. The invisible sandbags that I was accustomed to dragging around with me everywhere were gone! I felt like dancing into the store; it was amazing to have energy. I got choked up with tears because of the amount of joy I felt. It was such a relief to go grocery shopping without feeling like lying down in the aisles; I had forgotten what it felt like to be a normal person.

I had a new lease on life, and I could not wait to start living fully again. I started to dream and plan all the things I wanted to do and accomplish with a body that finally functioned properly.

I also remember going on a walk with Kayla one evening. It had been so long since I'd had the energy to go on a walk for fun, and it had been several years since I had been able to do that without feeling miserable the whole time. Once again, I felt like dancing as I went because I felt like a normal person. I could not believe the drastic change. It was like I had entered a heavenly realm, a return to pure bliss. I walked without pain; I walked without misery; I walked without being weighed down by fatigue.

We walked together around the neighborhood and then to the neighborhood park. We ran into my friend there, a friend whom we often passed there when we were driving in the car, when I did not have the energy to stop to let the children play. She was sitting on a bench when we approached her, and Kayla ran off to play with the children while I stood and talked to my friend. I was in awe that I could stand there and talk to her without desperately wanting to sit or lie down. I felt like a normal mom at the park.

It is impossible to explain the euphoria I experienced that day, the respite from all my problems and pain. That must be what heaven feels like, total and complete contentment.

Another joyful experience happened when I dropped Kayla off at a basketball practice one evening. The practice was at an elementary school. The gym was in the back part of the school, so I did not want to send Kayla in alone to weave through the dark hallways to get to the practice. Normally getting out of the car to help was something I dreaded, but that was not the case this time. I noticed how great I felt as I got out to lead the way. We had arrived at the school a little late, and since I was feeling well, I said, "Let's run!"

She did not hesitate. We ran quickly through the parking lot, into the school, and then through the halls together. Kayla dribbled her ball as we ran. My heart pounded with joy, along with the dribble of the ball. My heart felt like it would burst from happiness. I felt like I could run forever and that my limits were released. It felt so amazing that when I came back at the end of the practice to pick her up, I yearned to run again. I ran from the car to the school and then ran through the halls to pick her up. I felt a lump in my throat from the emotions that welled up from the joy of having a body that finally functioned well again.

I remember lying down in my bed at night, so happy to have enjoyed a day of energy and productivity. It had been so long since I had been able to feel well while going about my day. As I lay there on my back thinking about my blessings, I felt an intense gratitude that overwhelmed my body, causing tears of sheer joy to stream down the sides of my face. Oh, how I had missed the simple joys of a healthy body.

Once again, I was ready to shout from the rooftops that I was healed, and once again I was glad that I did not. It did not take long for my bad health to return, and I started reacting even worse to food despite my dedication to the diet. The more I took salicylates out of my diet, the more sensitive my body became. After experiencing a well-working body and getting my hopes up so high, I felt despair in returning to my sickly self. I was crushed.

After more research on the diet, I learned that eliminating salicylates can, in fact, backfire after a while and make a person even more sensitive to food. It became apparent that reintroducing salicylates into my diet would be beneficial so that my body would be inured to those food items. My body needed to get used to salicylates again. Although my body would still react to salicylates if I did that, at least I would not be hyper-sensitive to those foods.

Sure enough, when I started eating more salicylates, my hyper-sensitivity to foods improved. Yet, I was so discouraged. Once again, after thinking I found the cure to my problems, my hopes were dashed to pieces. I would do anything to enjoy a healthy body again. I had experienced just enough of a taste of a return to normalcy that it made me yearn for a healthy body even more.

I wished my body had a user's manual. The guessing game was so frustrating. I would do anything to improve my health, but I had no idea what the magical formula was. My unsuccessful search for answers left me crestfallen.

One night as I sat on the couch with Tyson watching television, despair hit full force. I found myself pleading with the Lord in my mind, yearning for relief. I let my thoughts sink into a dark place, deeper and deeper. Tears rolled down my face. I was overcome with an intense loss of hope. I told myself that life would not improve, that I would forever live in pain and misery.

Fear of my future overwhelmed every part of me, when all of the sudden an unfamiliar pain hit. It felt like a mild heart attack. The strange pain in my chest scared me. I immediately told Tyson we needed to get to the emergency room. He quickly called his parents, Delmar and Luann, to come watch the children so we could take off.

As we waited for them to arrive, although I was worried about my heart, I also felt a glimmer of hope. I was optimistic that this episode was an answer to that night's prayer. I thought surely whatever was happening to me was a culmination of my health problems and would finally help the doctors diagnose my condition. For that reason, I was relieved to be having this new pain. Surprisingly, the pain gradually subsided and was pretty much gone by the time my in-laws arrived.

I explained to Delmar and Luann what had happened, and Luann recognized the symptoms. She told me that I probably had a panic attack. Then she explained what panic attacks are and how they happen. I should have been relieved that it was just a panic attack, but once again, I was left without any answers to my long-term health problems. What I thought was an answer to my prayer was just my body's negative reaction to my distress.

I knew God could see how the lines and shapes of my design could come together in a pleasing way, so I wondered why I was left to flounder. I wanted His help to adjust the design of my life, but my search for answers only seemed to lead to dead ends.

9

EMERGING BEAUTY

I hated that my bad health kept me from accomplishing the goals that I had envisioned myself achieving. Months turned into years, and I felt like I would never be the person I wanted to be. Those brushstrokes in my life's painting did not make sense to me. Those colors were so ugly and did not seem to belong. I had a daily mental battle against the trial. I prayed and prayed for God to change my circumstances. This was not the plan I had for my life!

One morning, I felt sick as usual, and I laid suffering on the couch in our living room. A couple of the children were at home, entertaining themselves in the same room as me. That average day became one of the most important days of my life.

The heavens opened, and the Spirit taught me a vital lesson. Knowledge flowed through the Holy Ghost, insight I would not have thought of myself. It felt like the compilation of all those years of illness and pain had put me in the perfect state to hear this message from the Lord, loud and clear.

Specific thoughts and impressions filled my mind. The first feeling that poured over me was an unmistakable nearness to the Savior. My heart brimmed with His love. I felt the comfort and warmth of the Holy Ghost envelope me. I savored that feeling and yearned for it to stay.

Immediately following that sweet experience, the Spirit revealed to me that I had drawn closer to the Savior during that time of my life than I ever had before. Then it hit me with exceeding force that the reason I had drawn so near to the Savior was because of the intense trial I was undergoing. My strong connection to the Son of God was a direct result of the hardship I was facing.

At that moment, I could see that He had been with me all along, endowing me with His strength to endure. Consistently reaching out to him through prayer had blessed me in ways I had not seen. My trial helped me become more humble, patient, meek, and able to endure hardship. All those times of feeling all alone in my suffering had connected me to Him as I continually sought His help and guidance.

Like a bolt of lightning, I was enlightened, seeing there was indeed a purpose for my trial. It was not for naught! I celebrated inwardly at this revelation. My trial strengthened my relationship with my Savior, helping me draw nearer unto Him and to become more like Him.

I was overjoyed to see the brushstrokes of my painting take form. There was beauty emerging amidst the colors that had looked so disgusting to me. My trial was necessary, facilitating my unequivocal bond with Jesus Christ. I was so grateful that the Spirit gave me the gift of being able to see the change that the Savior facilitated.

The building of that relationship with my Savior triumphed over anything else I could have accomplished with a healthy body and a life devoid of strife. My trial must have been crucial enough for my spiritual development that it was worth it to God for me to miss out on so many of my other righteous desires. There were so many things I could have done to serve and bless my family's life and the lives of countless others if I had been healthy. Therefore, my trial must have been essential enough to my eternal progression that it was worth forfeiting those other worthwhile aspirations.

Earthly achievements that I yearned to obtain were menial in the eternal scheme of things. I would never be a basketball star, and I would never win mother of the year, and that is okay. Instead, I could be purified and perfected through the Atonement of Jesus Christ.

My spiritual rebirth was of everlasting consequence. Through His grace, I could emerge as a new creature. He could change my heart, reform my desires, alleviate my pride, and help me overcome the natural man. That is why I came to earth, for my spirit to be transformed and to continually progress toward eternal life.

My physical condition made it impossible to check off my to-do list of things that, in my mind, would perfect me. Fortunately, life is NOT a to-do list to get into heaven. Rather, it is a process of becoming more like the Savior. It is not the daily tasks we complete that perfect us. We do not become perfected by being the best cook, seamstress, housekeeper, or gardener. We do not even become perfected by reading the scriptures every day, developing our talents, or by being amazing at a church calling. We become perfected through Christ. It would not matter if I got all my to-do list accomplished in this life if, in the end, it did not produce a change of heart.

I am not saying that we should not strive to do the things on our spiritual to-do lists. Oftentimes those righteous acts are what create the change in our hearts. The Lord gives us commandments and instructions, not so we can merely check them off the list. He gives us that guidance because He knows that following those precepts will transform our spirits.

When we serve others and keep the commandments, we are blessed with increased faith and spiritual light. If we cannot fulfill all that He asks because of our trials and physical limitations, He will compensate for what we lack. The Atonement of Jesus Christ will fill in the gaps as we pray for help and as we try our best to live worthily.

D. Todd Christofferson said, "Where we can act, where we have the capacity and the means, we must act if we are to retain a justified and sanctified status. But where we legitimately and truly cannot act, the Lord will accept the desire for the deed."[1]

There are also times when accomplishing items on our spiritual to-do lists reflects that change that is being made in our hearts. Our desire to serve and keep the commandments grows as our love for the Lord increases. Our intent changes from wanting to obey just because we are supposed to, to wanting to obey because it brings us joy to follow Him. We want to demonstrate our love and gratitude for all He's done for us.

As a change of heart happens, the masterpiece of our lives takes form and becomes a work of beauty. And it is often our trials and our weaknesses that humble us, bring us to our knees, and make it possible for the enabling power to create that change in us. Heavenly Father wants us to change, not just to act.

Dallin H. Oaks said, "The Final Judgment is not just an evaluation of a sum total of good and evil acts–what we have *done*. It is an acknowledgment of the final effect of our acts and thoughts–what we have *become*."²

Somehow my spirit miraculously transformed due to negative circumstances. I was filled with charity, the pure love of Christ. I felt humbled and willing to do whatever was required of me. I noticed that because of my trial, I gained a strong confidence that my spirit is stronger than the natural man. When I thought my trial was keeping me from becoming who I wanted to be, I was actually becoming who the Lord wanted me to be through the gift of His grace.

The Spirit expanded my understanding that day, and I knew those insights were ones I would never want to forget. Despite my lack of energy, I immediately got off the couch and went straight to our computer. I did not want to forget the words and feelings that the Spirit had put into my mind and soul, so I quickly typed out the thoughts and impressions I had received.

Gratitude filled my heart that Heavenly Father was aware of me and willing to teach me a personal lesson that I desperately needed to hear. I felt like a conduit as the words poured from heaven, through my mind, and onto my journaling page.

From that day on, I recognized that I am clay in the Master Potter's hands. The pushing, pulling, pressing, squeezing, and twisting that left me feeling so wounded and inflicted upon, actually molded me into the beautiful vessel He always knew I had the potential to become. The pain and strain that I thought was crushing me and ruining my ability to be utilized, made me into something more ornate and spiritually functional than I could have ever imagined.

He knew my value and divine potential so well that He could not just leave me there as a lump of clay. He knew the pressure I would be subjected to would feel unbearable. He knew how miserable and abandoned I would feel. Surely it pained Him so much to see me hurting. I imagine Him weeping at my pain, wanting more than anything to relieve me of my anguish, knowing exactly how much I was suffering. He knew because He had felt my agony Himself.

Yet, He also knew I needed to experience those things and that the suffering would be worth it. I do not think the Savior caused my trials, but I do think He let me experience them because of the way those trials, as I came unto Him, helped me become His masterpiece.

Not long after receiving that divine inspiration about my trials, I heard an analogy by Linda S. Reeves that correlated so well with the lesson God had taught me. She helped me to see even more clearly that my trials have significance and purpose. She said:

> Almost three years ago, a devastating fire gutted the interior of the beloved, historic tabernacle in Provo, Utah. Its loss was deemed a great tragedy by both the community and church members. Many wondered, Why did the Lord let this happen? Surely He could have prevented the fire or stopped its destruction.
>
> Then months later, during the October 2011 general conference, there was an audible gasp when President Thomas S. Monson announced that the nearly destroyed tabernacle was to become a holy temple—a house of the Lord!
>
> Suddenly we could see what the Lord had always known! He didn't cause the fire, but He allowed the fire to strip away the interior. He saw the tabernacle

as a magnificent temple—a permanent home for making sacred eternal covenants.³

I discovered that during my experience in the refiner's fire, when I felt like I was "figuratively (being) burned to the ground," my Heavenly Father was actually rebuilding me into a "magnificent temple where His Spirit can dwell eternally."⁴

He is molding us in ways that we often cannot see or understand. We need to be willing to let go and trust, and then beauty will emerge, in His timing.

10

GOD'S TECHNIQUES

The revelation that God gave me buoyed me up and helped me face my trials with more hope and understanding. Knowing that God's skillful techniques were, in fact, transforming me into His masterpiece made my trials easier to face with faith. I was more willing to suffer in order to grow closer to the Savior.

I saw that my spirit was changing, but I was not sure exactly how it was done. Then I had the opportunity to hear Sheri Dew speak at a women's conference, and her message helped me see spiritual transformation in a whole new light.

Sheri Dew taught about the grace of Jesus Christ. It was a topic I had never thought much about. Up until that point, I had always heard grace referred to as regarding forgiveness of sins. I knew that because of Christ's grace we can all be forgiven of our sins if we repent, but I did not know much beyond that. She opened my eyes to an additional meaning, and it changed my life.

Sister Dew taught that grace is an enabling power. An

enabling power is any kind of divine help or strength that we receive through the power of Jesus Christ, made available through His Atonement. It is divine intervention and assistance.[1] I love the idea of having His power and strength available in my life.

The word *enable* means to make able or possible; to give power, means, competence, or ability.[2] Therefore, it makes sense that this enabling power is how the Savior bestows His power on us, making us more able and competent.

Sheri Dew gave an example from her life of how this enabling power made it possible for her to forgive her father. When she was growing up, her father had severe anger issues and was verbally abusive. She harbored a lot of ill feelings toward him because of that. Then, when her father was on his deathbed, she prayed on his behalf. As she prayed, the aching in her heart miraculously melted away and was replaced by a pure love for her father.[3]

The hurt that she had felt for so many years was beyond her own ability to surmount. It is through the grace of Jesus Christ that we have the power to overcome the feelings, trials, and shortcomings that we cannot conquer on our own. A change of heart is made possible through this enabling power. We can become new creatures through the Atonement of Jesus Christ.

The grace of Jesus Christ can transform us, making us *more capable*—more capable of overcoming temptation, more capable of overcoming the natural man, more capable of forgiving others, more capable of dealing with trials, more capable of having faith, more capable of loving others, and the list goes on and on.

That is what it means in Ether 12:27 when it says, "My grace is sufficient for all men that humble themselves before me; for if they humble themselves before me, and have faith in me, then will I make weak things become strong unto them."

After learning about the enabling power of grace, I realized I had been looking at the Atonement of Jesus Christ all wrong. At one time, I had heard grace described using an analogy of filling a glass with water. In that analogy, we as God's children, because we are mortal and very imperfect, try as we may, we can only fill up the glass with a certain amount of water. Then, after all we can do, the Savior finishes filling the glass.

After learning about grace, I now see that the analogy is a little flawed. The Savior does not just step in at the end to fill up our glass. Rather, if we, through prayer, are consistently inviting the Lord into the process of our lives, He will *continually* help us fill our glass full, even to overflowing.

Brad Wilcox said, "Grace is not a booster engine that kicks in once our fuel supply is exhausted. Rather, it is our constant energy source. It is not the light at the end of the tunnel but the light that moves us through the tunnel. Grace is not achieved somewhere down the road. It is received right here and right now."[4]

The Savior can be with us, helping us throughout life's journey. He can make our weaknesses strong, and He can make our strengths stronger.

After learning about grace, I now grasp an additional insight regarding the water in the glass analogy. Yes, the Savior can help us all along the way as we are filling our glass, but His enabling power can *also* make *us* more capable of filling our glass. Through Him, our water will not run out but will continually flow.

Up until my health trials, I viewed the Atonement of

Christ much like the inaccurate water in the glass analogy. I thought it was up to me to fill up my glass on my own as much as possible with my good deeds, will power, and righteous living. I had confidence that I could accomplish all that was needed for me to fill up my glass enough that on judgment day Christ would say, "Wow, nice job! Look how full you filled up your glass. You were not perfect, but because you repented along the way, I will fill up the rest of your glass. Off you go to the Celestial Kingdom!"

It took becoming incapable physically for me to realize that I cannot save myself.

Without having the abilities that I thought I would have to reach as high as I could for perfection, I had to turn to my Savior. It was only then that I learned that it was not my spiritual and temporal achievements that would get me into heaven, and I did not need to rely on my own strength and willpower to get me through this life. It was the grace of Jesus Christ that would change my spiritual being. He can strengthen me beyond my own capabilities. He can make more of me than I could ever be on my own.

I realized I can truly become like Him, but not just through my own works. His enabling power enhances my capacities, abilities, and spiritual strength beyond my own. Through the Atonement of Jesus Christ, I gain spiritual gifts of godly attributes, helping me become like the Savior.

Christ's grace can transform us, bestowing gifts of the Spirit on us. When we feel like it is beyond our own capacity to overcome the natural man and develop certain attributes, we need to seek the power of grace to help us attain those spiritual gifts.

I have heard some people blame their sins on the natural man, saying, "That is just the way I am."

If we truly understand the grace of Jesus Christ, we know that we can pray to God to transform our weaknesses into strengths. We need to seek out and pray for those gifts that will perfect us.

Although it is important to overcome the natural man, we should not rely on our own willpower to improve. We should seek the Savior's grace to endow us with His strength to progress. In the same way, we should not rely on our own ability to get through adversity.

Anthony Perkins said, "I fear that too many Church members think if they are just a little tougher, they can get through any suffering on their own. This is a hard way to live. Your temporary strength can never compare to the Savior's infinite supply of power to fortify your soul." He continued, "Whatever the cause of your sufferings, your Heavenly Father can direct them to refine your soul."[5]

Learning about grace helped me realize that His power is available to me in far-reaching ways, not just as a means to be forgiven of my sins. That knowledge motivated me to seek Him in all aspects of my life, especially when I feel weak and inadequate.

I realized that in my quest for a miracle of physical healing, I was instead endowed with spiritual miracles through the grace of Jesus Christ. I wanted my body to be healed, but God mended my spirit, transforming me into something better than I had envisioned for myself.

These miracles became more apparent when I heard a talk by David A. Bednar called, "Bear Up Their Burdens with Ease." He taught about the story in the Book of Mormon when Alma and his people were being persecuted by Amulon.

Mosiah 24:8 says, "Amulon began to exercise authority over Alma and his brethren, and began to persecute him, and cause that his children should persecute their children." Amulon forced Alma and his people do slave labor, and he threatened to kill them if they prayed to God. Since they could not pray out loud, they "... did pour out their hearts to him."

The Lord heard their inner pleadings and answered by saying, "And I will also ease the burdens which are put upon your shoulders, that even you cannot feel them upon your backs."[6]

Elder Bednar points out that hearing those words from the Lord makes you assume that the Lord will provide a miracle by immediately taking away the burdens of His people.[7]

That is exactly the way I expected my prayers to be answered during my health trial. I had faith that my trial would be removed.

However, Bednar recounts that in the next verse, the people are told that instead of having their burdens lifted, their burdens would be *eased*.[8]

"And now it came to pass that the burdens which were laid upon Alma and his brethren were made light; yea, *the Lord did strengthen them* that they could bear up their burdens with ease, and they did submit cheerfully and with patience to all the will of the Lord."[9]

Alma and his followers were strengthened through the enabling power of Jesus Christ to face their challenges. They were given the ability to have courage and fortitude to face their trials with faith, and their burdens were made light.

When I thought that being cured of my illness was key to creating my beautiful artwork, God knew better what would unlock my ultimate potential. His planned techniques would refine and add intricate detail, improving my canvas eternally. He knew the superior miracle would be to empower me to impact my circumstances.

Spiritual growth occurred as the Savior's grace gave me strength beyond my own to face my trial with patience and long-suffering.

11

FINDING THE MASTER PAINTER

When I was in middle school, my mom signed me up for a class with a master oil painter. This artist taught several students at once. I had never painted with oil paints before, so I relied heavily on her guidance throughout the class. I often reached a point in the painting process when I just had to stop and wait for the professional's help because I had no idea how to proceed without her personal instruction.

I remember being so frustrated during class because I spent so much wasted time looking around for her and waiting to receive one-on-one assistance. Sometimes, I would go looking for her, find her helping another student, and then wait next to her impatiently until she noticed I needed help. Eventually, I would receive her much-needed aid, but it did not come right when I wanted it.

The help of the Master Painter does not always come quickly, but His powerful expertise is always worth the wait. Sometimes His grace is attained a little at a time, and we are given just the necessary amount of strength to move forward. Even Christ grew grace by grace "until he received a fullness of the glory of the Father."[1]

There were times during my health struggles that His grace seemed out of reach. I felt abandoned when I wanted the help of the Master Painter so badly. I would plead for His presence and power, but I could not feel it there. I felt empty, wishing I could at least experience His comforting power. My prayers for strength to help me cope with the misery seemed unanswered.

Those sleepless nights, I would often resort to lying on the living room couch so I would not keep Tyson awake through my constant tossing and turning. As I lay there suffering, I sometimes quoted the song words in my mind, "Heavenly Father, are you really there? And do you hear and answer every child's prayer?"[2]

Tears rolled down my cheeks as I looked out the large windows into the dark night. I had not lost faith. I knew He was there. I just desperately yearned to feel His presence, to feel His love for me, but nothing came.

I had felt His comfort and strength so many times in my life, so why not now when I needed it more than ever? I still do not know all the answers to that question, but I do know that God works in mysterious ways.

Even the Savior felt abandoned by God as He hung on the cross and said, "My God, my God, why hast thou forsaken me?"[3] Christ in that moment did not question His Father's existence, He just questioned why He had to suffer alone.

Perhaps God does not come to our rescue right away so that we can feel the contrast between being empty and being filled with His love. We learn and grow from experiencing loneliness.

For example, we gain compassion and empathy for others who face difficulties. Also, great spiritual strength comes when we truly must rely on our faith in Him, knowing that He is there even when we cannot see or feel His presence. We learn to trust that the sun will rise again and that His light will return.

I love the insights S. Michael Wilcox shared about times in life when prayers seem unanswered. He told the story about Christ, found in both Mark 6 and Matthew 14.[4]

In that story, after Jesus fed the 5,000, He told His disciples to get onto a ship "to go to the other side," and He "departed into a mountain to pray."[5]

While Jesus was still on land, and the disciples were "in the midst of the sea," perhaps a metaphor for the disciples being faced with a difficult trial,[6] they were "tossed with waves: for the wind was contrary."[7]

Although Jesus ". . . saw them "toiling in rowing . . .," it was not until "the fourth watch of the night" that "Jesus went unto them, walking on the sea."[8]

Why would Jesus not go immediately to His disciples?

The disciples were struggling with a contrary wind and had been for a while. Jesus waited until the fourth watch of the night to come unto them.

It seems that sometimes the choppy sea of our lives is not calmed until after we have been tirelessly rowing against a contrary wind. We may feel as though we have been abandoned by the Lord, but He is always watching over us. As much as it must pain Him to not come to our rescue immediately, He lets us feel pain, loneliness, anger, heartache, and sorrow as a means of becoming more like Him.

Wilcox said, "When you feel somewhat desperate, when it seems like your prayers aren't answered and the winds still blow, take comfort in the knowledge that he is on the hillside watching. Remember, you might not know that he's watching as you struggle in the boat, but he is on the hillside watching, and he will come. But he generally comes in the fourth watch–after we have done all we can do."9

The Lord is aware of our suffering but knows that we need to struggle in order to reach our divine potential.

Macayle Stucki taught this concept, through an analogy on her Instagram page, @macaylestucki. Her two daughters never learned how to crawl because Macayle hated to watch them cry when she left them on their bellies. Even though Macayle's doctors advised her to leave them there for a while, she could not handle watching them struggle. She always rushed in to save them, so they never learned the valuable skill of crawling that would have allowed them to "experience and explore the world from their hands and knees." Macayle explained:

> Maybe that's why God doesn't always give us what we pray for. We'd miss out on a valuable skill, a skill that allows us to see and experience the world around us differently. It doesn't mean He's not there in the room with us. It doesn't mean He doesn't love us. Maybe He just knows what we're capable of, and He's giving us opportunities to reach for it. I've said some prayers that I thought went unanswered; but maybe God's answer was the same thing I plead in my heart when I see my babies struggle on their bellies. Maybe when I asked God for peace, and it did not come, He was exclaiming, *you can do this. Keep going. I'm here, but I won't hold you yet. I love you. Please keep struggling. You can do this.*

Ultimately, it's that struggle that develops muscles and the ability to crawl. Maybe when I call out to God and do not feel/see/hear what I ask for, it's not because

Heaven's silent, or God has left the room, or I've left God's room, but because, unlike me, God is a perfect parent who knows when to allow the struggle. Instead of holding me close in that moment, He's giving me a gift of growth and ability that I will cherish every day.[10]

Growth comes through difficulties that stretch us out of our comfort zone. God lets us experience those hardships even though they cause us discomfort.

When we feel alone in our suffering, we can be confident that He is nearby and knows of our pain. He is allowing us to learn and grow.

So, what should we do when we feel like God has abandoned us and that we have been left to face the contrary winds on our own?

As M. Russell Ballard has told us, we need to stay on "the Old Ship Zion," and "always wear a life jacket, and hold on with both hands."[11]

In other words, keep going to church, keep following the words of the Lord found in the scriptures and from the apostles and prophets. Never stop praying, keep trying, and do not give up.

We need to hold tightly to the iron rod even when we feel alone in our suffering. That is how we can find our way through the darkness.

Juventa Vezzani told how she clung to gospel truths to find her way through dark times of her life. She said:

"As I pondered Lehi's dream, I had a piercing realization. . ... Traveling through mists of darkness is a completely normal part of God's plan. He allows us to experience difficulties from time to time so that we can completely depend on Him and His Son. The key is to cling to the iron rod. I still saw myself in the mists of darkness, but I had hope."[12]

She went on to say:

"I began to immerse myself in the scriptures. I still had my dark days, but I had faith that if I clung to the iron rod--the word of God (see 1 Nephi 11:25)--I would be freed from the mists of darkness. I'm not sure how long it took, but one day I could at last taste of God's love again. It was like warm sunshine after a long winter."[13]

We may have to wait until the fourth watch, but answers *will* come, peace *will* be found, and Christ *will* give us the strength to overcome.

We should repeatedly seek out the Master Painter and patiently trust that He is there and that His guidance will come. Little by little, we will perceive glimpses of His influence in our paintings. Eventually, His impact will be indisputable when we see the stunning creation take form.

12

ACCESSING THE SAVIOR'S PALETTE

The Savior is waiting to bless us with His grace, but we need to come unto Him to access His divine, powerful palette.

I love the artistic depiction of Christ where He is at the door waiting to help us, but the doorknob is not on His side of the door.[1] We are the ones who need to open the door to invite Him in. Prayer is one way we can invite His influence and power into our lives. As we seek and ask for His help through prayer, His power can be manifest.

For example, one time I was hurt so deeply by something a friend said to me that I could not rid myself of the ache I felt in my heart. It was such a deep emotional pain that I tossed and turned that night, trying to no avail to push out the thoughts and feelings. It was not a feeling I was intentionally holding onto out of hostility toward the other person. Like Sheri Dew, I had a great desire to forgive that person and to get that horrible feeling out of me, but it was beyond my own capacity to get those negative feelings out of my mind and heart.

I realized that the only way to relieve my agony was to pray for access to His grace to help me forgive when I did not have the ability myself. I pleaded through prayer to be freed of the negative feelings that darkened my soul. I rarely have immediate answers to my prayers, but this was one of those times.

As soon as I ended my prayer, peace filled my heart, and my mind was put at ease. Turmoil was replaced by calm serenity. I could physically feel the change as the power of the Atonement lifted my burden and took the anger out of my soul.

Within a matter of minutes, I drifted off to sleep in the peace that only the Savior could bring. Not only did I sleep well that night, but I was able to forgive and forget the whole incident because of that desperate prayer for help.

Peace through the Atonement of Jesus Christ is something I never take for granted anymore, and I pray for it often when life gets tumultuous and distressing. Answers do not always come quickly. Sometimes I am left to feel anger, sadness, anxiety, or hopelessness for a while, but eventually the Savior's Atonement relieves me of those negative emotions, replacing them with a forgiving heart and a feeling of peace and hope.

Another means of accessing Christ's grace is through faith. We need to have faith in the Savior's power to change us.

Romans 5:2 says, "We have access by faith into this grace."

The story of Peter walking on water is a perfect example of accessing God's power with faith. That event was a continuation of the story I mentioned previously, when the Savior waited until the fourth watch to come unto them. When He finally came to the rescue, He did so by walking on the water toward them.

At first, the disciples were scared because they did not recognize the Savior. Then Peter said, "Lord, if it be thou, bid me come unto thee on the water." The Savior replied, "Come."[2]

Peter was such a great example of faith. He did as the Savior asked and stepped out onto the water to walk to Him. Peter knew his own deficiencies. He knew that if left to his own abilities and power, he would sink into the sea. He had faith that through the Savior's grace, he would be given the power he needed in that moment. He was full of faith, and looking unto Christ, he was given the power to walk on water.

Then Peter noticed the harsh winds of the storm around him. As soon as fear and doubt set in, he began to sink. He cried out to the Savior, "Lord, save me."

Matthew 14:31 tells us, "And immediately Jesus stretched forth his hand, and caught him, and said unto him, O thou of little faith, wherefore didst thou doubt?"

Peter was able to access Christ's power when he had faith, but when he let doubts and fear take over, that power was no longer there.

Gene R. Cook said, "The moment Peter doubted and took his eyes off the Savior, he severed himself from the power of Jesus Christ that had sustained him on the water. How many times, likewise, as we have prayed for assistance or help with our problems, have we severed ourselves from the power of God because of doubt or fear, and thus could not obtain this enabling power of God? (See D&C 6:36; D&C 67:3.)."[3]

In my life, there was one time in particular when I really had to have faith in God and, like Peter, trust that the Savior would buoy me up in a way that seemed impossible if left to my own devices. My sickness was at its worst, and I desperately wanted even just a little reprieve from the suffering. I had been searching and searching for answers, anything to bring a little relief from the pain, and the doctors were stumped. They could not figure out why I felt so sick all the time. They knew my sinuses hurt a lot, but they did not think a CT scan of my sinuses would be worth the radiation risks. For some reason, they seemed sure that my sinuses were not the source of the problem.

Finally, I came across a doctor who thought, since my sinuses were the only blaring possible culprit, that it was worth the risks to get a CT scan. Feeling desperate, I followed her advice. Those scans ended up revealing that my sinuses were almost totally full of chronically infected tissue. I took those results back to the doctor who had told me I did not need the scan, and he said "Wow, your sinuses are impressive, in a bad way." He then told me that he rarely suggests sinus surgery, but that I should definitely look into it.

I went home and immediately started researching sinus surgery. The more research I did, the more excited I got. If I got all that garbage cleared out of my sinuses, maybe the infections would stop. And maybe getting rid of the chronic infections would alleviate, or at least improve, my body pain and fatigue as well. My hopes soared as I read success story after success story. I was ecstatic!

I then went to a sinus specialist, so ready for him to heal me and for all my problems to end. The doctor looked at my scans, and to my surprise, immediately started listing all the reasons that sinus surgery would not benefit me.

He said in people with my particular symptoms, the problem returns soon after surgery, not making it worth the surgery risks. Then he listed all the scary risks of the surgery and offered no alternative treatment to help me.

The more he talked, the more my heart sank. It took

everything I had to not start crying. I could not say much back to the doctor in my attempt to keep the tears from coming. I'm sure he had no idea how devastating it was for me as each word he spoke smothered all my hope of getting relief from years of misery.

I hurried out of his office feeling totally dejected and empty and could not wait to get into my car so I could let the floodgates open.

I got in my car, tears rolling down my face, overcome with the worst feeling of hopelessness that I had ever felt. Like Peter, at that moment all I could see was the tumultuous storm around me. The winds were too strong. My circumstances were too difficult. My ability to endure was inadequate. I lost sight of the Savior.

I sat in that parking lot for a while, thinking, how can I go on with no hope for relief? I felt like I hit a dead end. How could I keep enduring the suffering? I started sinking.

In that darkest moment, I spiritually caught sight of the Savior's outreached hand, catching me, and saying, "O thou of little faith, wherefore didst thou doubt?"[4]

My faith returned as I symbolically took His hand. Knowing that I was not left to my own power, saved me that day from drowning in the boisterous sea.

My despair quickly turned into hope as I thought of the knowledge I have that God loves me and that through Christ I would be able to handle any suffering that lay ahead. I know that God is all-powerful and could and would take away my trial if it was not going to benefit me. I am His child, and He wants what is best for me. I felt myself lay my problems at the feet of the Savior, having faith that everything would be all right, no matter the outcome. Having my foundation built on Christ saved me from crumbling and has saved me many times since.

I have faith that God works miracles in our lives. Sometimes He will miraculously take a trial away, but more often, the miracle is Him giving us the strength to endure the trial well. He helps us walk on water while the storm rages all around us. If we want God's grace to aid us in our trials, we need to have faith.

Although grace requires our faith, Heavenly Father also requires us to do all in our own power. He expects us to do our part.

Doctrine & Covenants 123:17 says, "Therefore, dearly beloved brethren, let us cheerfully do all things that lie in our power; and then may we stand still, with the utmost assurance, to see the salvation of God, and for his arm to be revealed."

We need to do our part by striving to keep the commandments. Righteous living qualifies us for His grace. We do not need to be perfect, but we need to be trying. I love this quote by George Q. Cannon. He said:

> "Obedience to the Gospel brings [people] into very close and intimate relationship with the Lord. It establishes a close connection between men on the earth and our Great Creator in the heavens. It brings to the human mind a feeling of perfect confidence in the Almighty and in His willingness to listen to and answer the supplications of those who trust Him. In times of trial and difficulty this confidence is beyond price. Trouble may come upon the individual or upon the people, disaster may threaten and every human hope may seem to be overthrown, yet, where [people] have availed themselves of the privileges which obedience to the Gospel brings, they have a sure standing

place; their feet are upon a rock that cannot be moved."⁵

During that difficult day, when all my hopes were crushed when the doctor told me that sinus surgery would not benefit me, my faith and confidence quickly returned because of my knowledge that I was obeying the commandments. Because I knew I was obeying gospel principles to the best of my ability, I knew that Heavenly Father would bless me with whatever was best for me. He was aware of me, and He was listening to my prayers. I was not perfect, but I knew I was making a valiant effort.

I also knew that I was doing all in my own power to remedy the situation. It was such a great comfort to know that my suffering was not a result of my disobedience. Obedience brought great confidence that the power of God would assist me. I knew I could trust Him and that I could put my life in His hands.

Living my life according to gospel principles gave me a sure foundation, built upon the Savior Jesus Christ. As we follow Him and keep His commandments, our testimonies will act as an anchor. With that anchor, life's challenges and the temptations of the world will not blow us off-course.

We do not need to be perfect to access Christ's grace, but we need to do our best to repent of our sins when we fall short.

Gene R. Cook stated, "A repentant heart and good works are the very conditions required to have grace restored to us. When someone pleads fervently in prayer for an answer, the answer may be more conditioned on repentance of personal sins than on any other factor."⁶

Humility also gives us access to the grace of the Savior.

Ether 12:27 (previously mentioned) tells us that, through the Savior's grace, our weaknesses can become strengths if we humble ourselves before Him and have faith in Him. We need to overcome pride and realize that we need the Atonement of Jesus Christ. Often the purpose of our trials is to humble us so that we turn to Heavenly Father and ask for His help.

I picture God waiting in heaven with power available to bestow on each of us. I am sure He often must wait until we are going through a difficult trial to extend that power to us, because that is when we humbly, sincerely, and diligently pray and ask for it. God has blessings He wants to bestow on us, but they "are made conditional on our asking for them."[7]

When life is uncomplicated, we tend to forget to humbly ask for His guidance and strength. It is easy at those times to think we are doing fine on our own.

Instead, we should constantly be seeking His direction and help. My prayers become much more consistent and fervent when trials have humbled me. I realize how much I need God's hand in my life and that I do not want to face life's difficulties without His assistance and support. I seek added blessings and strength when my own strength is depleted.

I was brought into the depths of humility through my health trial. Gaining God's power sounded so appealing to me because I was so weak on my own. That young girl who wanted to win every game of Monopoly, now did not care about "winning" in life. I was not competing against anyone anymore. I just wanted to make it through. I wanted to strive to the best of my ability, to be strengthened to endure well, and to cross the finish line.

I learned that God helps all who come unto Him to cross the finish line together if we are striving to move in the right direction.

I have heard it said that God will not give us more than we can handle, but I do not think that is completely true. I think that sometimes we are given more than we can handle on our own so that we are humbled enough to turn to God for help.

We seek His grace when we realize our own palettes are limited and that the colors the Savior has to offer will enhance and ultimately perfect our palettes.

When we turn to Him, He will endow us with His power so that we can make it through, with His help, what we could not otherwise handle on our own.

13

ETERNAL RULES OF COMPOSITION

Like artistic rules of composition, God has laws that, when followed, will create an optimal design that will help us grow and progress on our path to eternal life. Following His laws brings joy, even amidst hardship. As we make covenants with God to follow His laws, He blesses us in our artistic endeavors, helping us pattern our paintings after His.

Covenant keeping makes all the blessings of the Atonement of Jesus Christ available in our lives. One of those blessings is the gift of grace, His strength and power.

Doctrine and Covenants 109:22 tells us that we receive strength and power in God's temple:

> "And we ask thee, Holy Father, that thy servants may go forth from this house armed with thy power, and that thy name may be upon them, and thy glory be round about them, and thine angels have charge over them."

That is a compelling reason to attend the temple and to strive to keep the covenants that are made there. I want to attend the temple and be armed with power and glory, with angels having charge over me.

The power that we receive in the temple is the priesthood power of God. That power is endowed on both men and women as covenants are made and kept. We make promises to God, and as we keep those promises, God bestows his priesthood power on us.

Although women are not ordained to priesthood offices, the blessings of the priesthood are still available to them. I am just now learning that those who are ordained to the priesthood open the doors for priesthood power to be bestowed on both men and women. I love the way Neil L. Andersen explained it:

> "A man may open the drapes, so the warm sunlight comes into the room, but the man does not own the sun or the light or the warmth it brings. The blessings of the priesthood are infinitely greater than the one who is asked to administer the gift."[1]

Those ordained to the priesthood open the drapes so that both men and women can make covenants and obtain priesthood power in their lives. Russell M. Nelson said that keeping covenants binds us to the Savior.

> "His essential ordinances bind us to Him through sacred priesthood covenants. Then, as we keep our covenants, He endows us with His healing, strengthening power."[2]

I love the concept of being bound to the Savior. I feel so

weak alone, but I know I will make it through hard times with Him by my side.

What does it mean to bind ourselves to the Savior?

In the Savior's own words, He said, "Take my yoke upon you, and learn of me; for I am meek and lowly in heart: and ye shall find rest unto your souls. For my yoke is easy, and my burden is light."[3]

When two animals, like oxen, are used to pull a heavy load, a wooden beam or bar is placed across the animals to help them pull the load together. That wooden frame is called a yoke, and it helps them pull a load more efficiently as a team. It helps them stay side-by-side so they can move the same direction.

In the same way, Christ wants to join us by our side to help carry our burdens. Although the weight distribution is uneven because His power is so much greater than ours, He eagerly joins us in pulling when we yoke ourselves to Him through making and keeping covenants.

Emily Belle Freeman wrote about the idea of yoking ourselves to the Savior in a way I had not thought of before. She taught that it is essential as we strive to yoke ourselves to the Savior that we trust His will in our lives. She said:

> "The yoking becomes the trusting. Taking the yoke means I have allowed my heart to trust in Him, that I have let go of what holds me back—the fear, unmet expectation, the control. I let it all go when I take up the yoke. I agree to move in the direction He wants me to move. To turn the corners He wants to turn. To pull whatever weight He sees fit for me to pull. With Him."[4]

It is so hard to let go of what we want in life and to trust that the Lord's plan is better than what we have envisioned. Thinking about a yoke made me realize the importance of accepting our trials and being willing to not only put His yoke upon us but to accept His will and push in the same direction that He wants us to go.

I can picture a stubborn ox pulling away, yanking, trying so hard to go a different direction. That ox does not want to go through the trial and pull the heavy load. It wants to avert it somehow, but it gets nowhere as it struggles.

I have felt that way a lot in my life. I have yanked in an opposite direction mentally, wanting so badly for trials to be removed rather than accept them, rather than whole-heartedly strapping myself to the yoke and plowing straight ahead with His help, the direction He wants me to go.

We need to accept trials and plow through them. It is through accepting and moving in the same direction as the Lord's will that helps us carry our load, getting us where He wants us to go with His loving guidance.

I am sure we are foregoing blessings if we are not pushing forward according to the Lord's will.

Emily Belle Freeman said we often need to leave something behind we want in order to follow God's path. She assures us that "What lies in front . . . will always be better than what [lies] behind."[5]

That reminds me of a meme of a young girl who is holding tightly to her small teddy bear. Jesus is across from her, holding out His hand, gesturing for her to hand the teddy bear to Him.

The girl says, "But I love it, God."

What she does not see is that the Lord has a much larger, nicer teddy bear behind His back ready to give to her. She does not realize that giving up what she wants will end up bringing greater blessings.

Thinking about the yoke analogy also makes me think about the way yoking ourselves to Him can transform us in the process.

The more we pull alongside the Savior, the more capable we become ourselves. We are strengthened. We become new creatures through His infinite power. I picture Christ as the strongest, perfect ox, and as we pull alongside Him, although we are weak, our strength gradually increases over time. We become spiritually stronger little by little until eventually we are strong like Him.

It helps me see the need for adversity in our lives. If we did not have a load to pull, we might not see the need to yoke ourselves to Him, seeking His strength and power in our lives. Therefore, without the load, we would not gain that transformative power of grace He offers us.

I love an analogy our daughter Sierra wrote that teaches how covenants bind us tightly to God during adversity. She wrote about one of her favorite hobbies, rock climbing. She said:

> In rock climbing we tie a knot called a figure eight knot that keeps us securely tied in as we climb up. This knot is designed perfectly so that instead of loosening, the knot becomes even tighter when we stumble, make mistakes, and fall on the climbing wall, as long as we tie a complete figure eight knot.
>
> This same thing can happen as we are tied to God. We must consistently and thoroughly bind ourselves to God in order for His promises to remain sure. As we walk the covenant path, our trials and struggles can create a tighter bond with God and will help us stay connected and protected.

The covenant path is a path that will strengthen us and help us endure with faith as we know with surety that God knows us and is bound to His promises when we are obediently walking our path with Him.

As we make and keep covenants, we are tying the figure-eight knot, binding ourselves to God. The Savior said, "I, the Lord, am bound *when ye do what I say;* but when ye do not what I say, ye have no promise."[6]

I read a book my friend, Rex Young, wrote about his experiences as a caregiver to his wife as she suffered from dementia. It struck me what a great example he was of someone who put the yoke of the Savior upon him by not only keeping his covenants but accepting the will of the Lord and plowing through the difficulties.

His wife Marla was a hospice patient for almost five years, requiring his constant care, 24 hours a day, seven days a week. Reading about the nonstop, daily work, as well as the many mishaps associated with caregiving, made me feel like it must have been such a trying time. Yet, if it was difficult, you would not know it because of Rex's positive attitude.

Throughout the book, when something particularly positive would evolve on a specific day, he would write, "Today has been a very good day. Of course, every day is a good day but some days are better than others."[7]

I found that to be the overall theme of his caregiving experience, gratitude despite difficulties. There was no "woe is me, why did the Lord let this happen?" or dwelling on what life could have been like without his wife's dementia.

Instead, he kept his covenants, accepted God's will, and did not just find joy in the best days but found the good in every day. He showed gratitude and love in the face of adversity. His figure-eight knot was tied correctly, so his trials only secured his bond with God and with his wife. I love how Rex also wrote:

> "Although sometimes have been difficult, I have never considered it a burden to care for her. I have many memories that I will cherish forever. Yes today has been a very good day."[8]

I could list many similar quotes from his book. He's such a great example of accepting the Lord's will with a grateful heart. Rather than becoming angry or bitter, he pulled alongside the Savior and became more and more Christlike in the process. He kept His covenants joyfully.

In his author biography on the back of his book, it says, "His greatest accomplishment was providing loving care to his Sweetheart during her illness."

Another great example of the power of covenant keeping is Alma the elder's people mentioned previously. They had entered into the covenant of baptism, and, despite King Amulon's death threats, they found a way to keep their covenants by fervently praying to the Lord silently in their hearts.

The Lord heard and answered their prayers. Although they did not have their trials removed, their covenants had yoked them to the Savior. He helped them pull their load, and they received strength to carry on despite their hardships.[9]

I also love that in answer to their prayers, the Lord talked to them, saying: "Be of good comfort, for I know of the covenant which ye have made unto me."[10]

He let them know that He was aware of them, and that they could rest assured because of their covenant keeping.

That makes me think back to the priesthood blessing Tyson and our friend gave me. Although I did not receive the healing blessing that I desperately wanted, like Alma's people, hearing that the Lord was aware of me and that He would be there to strengthen me, brought me peace.

I needed to take His yoke upon me, stop trying to pull the other way, and let Him guide me in His way, and I would be blessed.

14

EMBRACING GOD'S METHODS

We can access the Savior's grace more fully when we accept God's will in our lives. We need to trust that our Creator's methods will make a masterpiece out of the brushstrokes of our lives.

Oftentimes, our trials do not make sense, and our lives take different turns than we expect or desire. We need to have faith that He, who knows all, will create something beautiful out of those unexpected and sometimes painful brushstrokes.

Jesus was the ultimate example of accepting the will of Heavenly Father when He was about to take upon Him the pain, sickness, and sins of all of us. He prayed, saying, "If it be possible, let this cup pass from me: nevertheless not as I will, but as thou wilt."[1]

Jesus prayed to be spared the pain and suffering, but He was ultimately willing to submit to the will of the Father.

I am a work in progress in striving to follow the Savior's example by aligning my will with God's. It is not easy, and I often fail and have to repent and realign. I have had so much faith that I can be healed, and I have prayed earnestly for that to happen. What I have had a harder time doing, is having faith that I can endure the trial if being healed is not His will for me.

The Lord knows what is best for us and our eternal progression.

Richard G. Scott said that Christ's invitation to, "Ask, and ye shall receive" (3 Nephi 27:29) does not assure that you will get what you *want*. It does guarantee that, if worthy, you will get what you *need*, as judged by a Father that loves you perfectly, who wants your eternal happiness even more than do you."[2]

The purpose of coming to earth is to become as He is, and the crucible of afflictions is necessary for this change to occur. We should trust that process, as painful as it is. If we are doing all in our own power, we can rest assured that the Lord will guide our path in His way. We can lay our problems at the feet of the Savior and trust that all will work out for our good. Some blessings may not come until the next life, but they will come.

I have had many discouraging thoughts over the years: Why can't I be a fun mom with lots of energy? Why can't I be a supportive wife who always has dinner on the table? Why can't I have a break from pain and discomfort? Those kinds of thoughts are counterproductive.

Carol Wilkinson said, "Rather than asking "why questions" we should ask questions such as, "What should I do?" or "What do you want me to learn from this?" Try to find out what the Lord's will is. Obviously, He wants you to be obedient to His commandments, but what else does He have in mind for you? Tell Him what your desires are, but be prepared to do His will."[3]

As we seek to know God's will rather than feeling

discouraged that our paintings are not turning out how we planned, He will direct our brushstrokes.

We should trust in God because He is omniscient, knowing the beginning and the end. He foresees the finished product and knows what we need to go through to achieve our optimal design. He knows our masterpiece will require some dark shadows and some messy brushstrokes in order to be perfected.

When I heard Gene Corson speak in church, he helped me understand that not only does submitting to the will of the Lord help us access Christ's grace, but it is also a means for us to personally give a gift to the Lord.

He said, "The one thing that we truly possess for ourselves and the only gift that we can actually give our Heavenly Father is when we are meek enough, humble enough, faithful enough and trusting enough to come before our Heavenly Father with a broken heart and a contrite spirit and say unto Him the four most important words we can ever say to Him, *Thy Will Be Done.*" He then quoted Neal A. Maxwell:

> "The submission of one's will is really the only uniquely personal thing we have to place on God's altar. The many other things we give to God, however nice that may be of us, are actually things He has already given us, and He has loaned them to us. But when we begin to submit ourselves by letting our wills be swallowed up in God's will, then we are really giving something to Him."[4]

I love that. That is the greatest gift we can give to God and the way we can show our gratitude for all He has given us. We can accept His will for our lives.

When we place our will on the altar, we show that we trust our Creator to make more of our lives than we can on our own.

Learning that concept brought me so much joy. It gave meaning to my suffering. I realized that coming to terms with my health problems was a way I could give a gift to God. Enduring my trials well, with meekness and grace, was a way I could demonstrate my love and devotion to Him.

As we consecrate our lives to God, we will be transformed.

For me, submitting my will to God's will did not mean that I stopped trying to find answers to my health problems, and it did not mean giving up hope. Instead, I gave myself permission to stop worrying about it, stressing about it, and feeling guilty about it. That was not doing any good. My gift to Him was to find peace in my circumstance—not letting pain and suffering cause bitterness, and having faith that God would consecrate my suffering for my good.

I needed to work on being humble and trusting God's will in my life. It is hard to let go and trust. I realized I should stop trying to wish the trial away. I had been having a mental battle each day against the trial. I was impatiently waiting for God to take the trial away. It was getting in the way of my plans for my life.

My wise friend Emily Spencer once advised me, "Sometimes strength and progress come first through acceptance of weakness and vulnerability. When you reach that point of just submitting yourself to it and accepting it, then you're willing to let go and trust. And when you start trusting, that's when amazing things happen."

I had to submit to the trial. I also needed to trust that "doing all I could do" was enough, even though I could do so little. I had to shift my way of thinking and shift my goals and make the best of my circumstances. Rather than having cookies waiting as the kids walked in from school, like my mom did, I had a hug and a smile waiting. Rather than having a list of things to accomplish during the day, I made simple goals of reading scriptures together and praying together.

I discovered that my job was to take each day at a time and do the best with what I was given. If that meant that I did not get anything done each day besides trying to have the best attitude possible, then that was enough. Even on the days I could not keep a positive attitude, it would still be enough because I could repent and try better the next day to submit my will to Him. I decided to strive each day to give the only gift I could truly give the Lord—my will. I would make the best of my circumstances rather than feeling self-pity.

It was freeing to succumb to the trial rather than fight it. When I did that, the paint flowed more freely as I let the Master Painter take control.

My attitude improved, and I felt more peace when I accepted my trial as my current "task" that God wanted me to fulfill. The part of my personality that loved to achieve goals, found new meaning in my trial when I was able to view my trial as the main item on my to-do list that I would be facing each day.

I told myself, *this is what I am supposed to be doing with my life right now. This is the current role God wants me to fulfill to the best of my ability. My goal is to be patient in my long-suffering.*

As easy as that sounded, I learned I had to be careful when giving myself permission to submit to the trial, that I did not give up all motivation to accomplish other things. Yes, there were days that I felt so awful that I needed to stay in bed and feel at peace about it, but there were also days that I needed to push myself enough to get necessary things done.

It became a bit of a tug of war as I tried to find a balance between being at peace with my illness, and pushing through the fatigue when necessary. Sometimes pushing myself through the pain was what was needed for that day, and getting up and moving improved my energy levels and my mood. Other times, I needed to give myself grace because my body did not cooperate with what I wanted to accomplish, and I could not push through the fatigue.

I prayed often to know God's expectations for me. I prayed to feel God's approval and to feel at peace in doing all I could do.

15

SAVORING THE CREATIVE PROCESS

Although producing artwork can be frustrating and difficult, there is always joy to be found in the creative process. We can have a spirit of gratitude no matter our circumstances, which is an important part of submitting to God's will.

I knew I needed to look for blessings amidst my hardships, which is not easy when life is painful. It is much easier to focus on the negative and to feel sorry for myself.

I am so glad I was given helpful advice about gratitude when I was a young mom. Experienced mothers told me to treasure the time I had with my young children. Those friends said that when they were in the middle of raising children, life felt so hard. Those long days felt like they would never end. Those moms looked forward to their children growing up and becoming more independent.

Those friends later wished they had appreciated those times more because looking back, those precious moments flew by. Their children grew up quickly and left home. Those mothers missed that time of life, and they wished they had not taken that time for granted. They even wished they could turn back time and relive those precious years.

Each phase of life has positive and negative aspects. Those positive aspects will one day be missed greatly and should therefore be cherished as much as possible in the moment.

Thomas S. Monson said, "I plead with you not to let those most important things pass you by as you plan for that illusive and nonexistent future when you will have time to do all that you want to do. Instead, find joy in the journey–now."[1]

It is a human tendency to look to the future to find happiness rather than finding joy in the present.

When I was a child, I looked forward to being old enough to get my driver's license. When I was in high school, I could not wait to be a college student. When I was in college, I hoped to get married. When I got married, I yearned to have children. I started to notice that not only did I look to the future to find happiness, I also looked back to the past and missed the happy, good times I had experienced previously.

It made me realize that I did not want to wait until each phase of life was over to acknowledge and appreciate the happiness and good in those phases. I wanted to find joy in my current circumstances.

Monson went on to quote Horace, the ancient Roman philosopher, "Whatever hour God has blessed you with, take it with grateful hand, not postpone your joys from year to year, so that in whatever place you have been, you may say that you have lived happily."[2]

I heard great advice from a young mother, my friend Kiley Hatch, in a talk she gave about gratitude. She taught that we should "savor" the positive aspects of our lives. She said:

I once heard of a gratitude exercise that is so simple, and yet so powerful. It's called *Savoring*. Pretend that you haven't eaten for two days, and someone puts one piece of your favorite candy in front of you. How would you eat that piece of candy? Would you swallow it whole without chewing just to get it quickly into your stomach? Or, more likely, would you take a bite, and notice intently on how it feels, smells, and tastes in your mouth before swallowing and taking another tiny bite in order to make the candy last as long as possible?

Savoring life is done in the same way. It is the capacity to notice, appreciate, and intensify the simple positive aspects during our day.

The next time you are at the dinner table with your family, notice each person. Imagine what it would be like if tomorrow they weren't there. Let yourself sink into that feeling. Or when you climb into bed at night, savor the feeling of comfort that settles over you from being warm under your covers. Or when you hear the sound of your children laughing in another room, listen to each laugh. Savor it and imagine what it will be like when they are all grown up and you won't hear their laughs flowing through your home all day.

That process of stopping, sinking in, and feeling can bring strong feelings of contentment and gratitude. Researchers have found that through continuously practicing the act of savoring, we can learn to live in a consistent state of gratitude.

I am so glad I savored the moments I had with our young children. Although I felt unwell physically much of the time, I tried my best to soak in my family's goodness and to enjoy their presence. When I spent a lot of time on the couch feeling sick, oftentimes one of my children would be cuddled up right next to me, and I loved that.

Having so much affectionate bonding time with them was something I would not have experienced if it were not for my health trials. I was regularly available to my children whenever they needed someone to talk to or to cuddle with. I have a sweet relationship with each of them because of that. I am glad I paid attention to those opportunities to savor the people I love.

There is definitely joy to be found amidst hardship. Sometimes that joy would not be seen or felt as strongly without the trial to illuminate how much there is to be grateful for.

Since I often did not have enough energy to be busy doing productive tasks, my trial gave me plenty of opportunities to watch our children grow up. I loved watching the creative ways they played with each other and with their friends. With our family being musically inclined, I spent a lot of time watching the children singing and dancing to music and making up their own songs. I also enjoyed listening to them practice their instruments.

To this day, listening to my children sing and play music is one of my sweetest joys in life. There were not many of their childhood moments that passed me by; I was right there watching and experiencing them. In that way, my trial was a blessing in disguise. I got to savor more than I ever would have otherwise.

I found that striving to foresee possible regrets helped me to observe the good around me. I did not want to look back and realize I was blind to all the beauty in my life. I did not want to neglect noticing and savoring the good mixed in with the bad. I would never get a chance to redo that time in my life. I would never get to raise our children again. I would never get to experience those special, unique stages that each of our children went through.

I decided to notice the special moments and to cherish the time I had with my husband and children, even though it was not the life I had envisioned. I could still offer them my best self under imperfect circumstances.

I asked myself, *how do I want to be remembered during these times of sickness? As a positive person or a negative person? As someone who loves those around me or as someone who pushes others away?*

If we wait until life is easy or free of challenges to find joy, life will pass us by and regrets will ensue. We need to be grateful in our current circumstances.

Dieter F. Uchtdorf said, "Being grateful in our circumstances is an act of faith in God. It requires that we trust God and hope for things we may not see. . . .. Being grateful in times of distress does not mean that we are pleased with our circumstances. It does mean that through the eyes of faith we look beyond our present-day challenges."[3]

I love Nephi's example of being grateful despite hardships. After being on a ship for several days in a terrible storm where his brothers tormented him and bound him with cords, he said, "I did look unto my God, and I did praise him all the day long; and I did not murmur against the Lord because of mine afflictions."[4]

I hope to imitate Nephi's example by praising God even during hardship.

One way I do this is with prayers of gratitude. During my nightly prayers, I find it helpful to think sequentially through the events of the day and thank Heavenly Father for each blessing I noticed.

I start by thinking of the positive aspects of that morning, then the afternoon, and then the evening. For example, my prayers will include things like, *I am so grateful I felt well enough to get out of bed in the morning to say goodbye to Tyson and the children before they left for work and school . . . I am so grateful I had the energy to go to the store today and to put the groceries away . . . I am grateful, since I did not feel well today, that I did not have any major obligations and that I could rest and nap . . . I am so grateful that I was able to make dinner for my family tonight . . .* etc.

Some days are easier than others to notice the good. On difficult days, my prayers of gratitude sounded more like, *I am grateful I was able to make it through this day.*

When blessings can't be immediately seen in our lives, we can still have an overall spirit of gratitude, a gratitude that supersedes our present circumstances. We should strive for a grateful heart, one that can praise God even when times are tough.

A testimony of the truths of the gospel can bring us great gratitude during the storms of life, bringing peace and hope in knowing God has a plan for us. We can have faith that God has great blessings in store for us, even eternal life with Him and our loved ones.

Knowing this mortal life is temporary and that it is merely a steppingstone to eternal glory and happiness can bring us immense gratitude no matter the trials we are going through.

Dieter F. Uchtdorf said, "In any circumstance, our sense of gratitude is nourished by the many and sacred truths we *do* know: that our Father has given His children the great plan of happiness; that through the Atonement of His Son

Jesus Christ, we can live forever with our loved ones; that in the end, we will have glorious, perfect, and immortal bodies, unburdened by sickness or disability; and that our tears of sadness and loss will be replaced with an abundance of happiness and joy."[5]

Although we do not always have control over our circumstances, we do have control over our attitude.

Viktor E. Frankl told in a book about his experience in a Nazi concentration camp. As you can imagine, he suffered extreme hardships due to the cruelty of his oppressors. Despite being forced into servitude and losing control of most aspects of his life, he was able to see life through a lens of gratitude.

He said, "Everything can be taken from a man but one thing: the last of the human freedoms–to choose one's attitude in any given set of circumstances, to choose one's own way."[6]

We can find purpose in our suffering. Even when we are deprived of the simplest joys of life, our lives still have direction and meaning. We can find purpose by seeking to prevail over our circumstances by having a positive outlook.

Life can still hold meaning for us because we can achieve the overarching goal of having a good attitude. We can triumph by not letting external forces bridle our mindset.

Our trials are often a test of how we will react to our circumstances. Will we focus on the negative or the positive? Will we choose despair or hope? Will we choose to turn away from God or toward God? Will we continue to keep our covenants?

16

JUST ENOUGH PAINT

As I sought to see the blessings amidst the difficult creative process, I noticed God answering my prayers in unexpected ways. Usually those answers came in small, almost imperceptible brushstrokes, adding just enough paint where needed, to sustain me in my time of need. Although I hoped for a miraculous healing, instead Heavenly Father provided small blessings to bolster me.

One summer, Tyson and I were asked to help with a pioneer handcart trek for some of the youth in our church. It is an event in which the youth pull handcarts and reenact some of the experiences of the pioneers who journeyed to the Salt Lake Valley in the mid-1800's. As part of the trek, I was asked to play the part of one of the pioneers named Mary Ann Mellor. I was invited to tell her faith-promoting story as if I were her.

On the second morning of the trek, the adult leaders decided to have me sneak ahead on the trail as the youth were preparing to pull their handcarts to the next destination.

When I got far enough ahead and found a good waiting spot, I prepared to do the reenactment. Then the youth started to make their way toward me with their handcarts.

When the youth caught up to me, they were surprised to find me sitting on the side of the trail eating a pie, pretending to be Mary Ann Mellor. They gathered around me as I told the story of Mary Ann, as if I were her. It was a hard story for me to tell without crying because I could see my own story reflected in hers.

Mary Ann had a very difficult time crossing the plains. Because of her health problems and extreme homesickness, she reached a point on the journey where she felt like she just could not go any farther. She sat down on a rock and cried, ready to give up.

Her family could not wait for her because they had to keep up with the rest of the handcart company. Mary Ann's daughter Louisa could not stand the thought of leaving her mother behind and alone, so she decided to stay with her mom.

When the company left, Louisa went to find a good spot to pray. She found a secluded area and prayed that her mom would have the strength of body and mind to catch up with the company.

As Louisa started walking back to her mom, she was amazed to find a pie sitting on the road! It was a miracle. She gave it to her mom who ate it happily.

The pie was just what Mary Ann needed to change her attitude, and it gave her the strength to keep going. Although Louisa's prayer on behalf of her mom was answered in a very unexpected way, it was just what Mary Ann needed at the time, getting her back on the trail.[1]

What struck me about this story was that the Lord did not take Mary Ann's trial away. Instead, He answered

Louisa's prayer in a way that gave Mary Ann the strength and optimism to keep going.

I related to Mary Ann because of the way my health problems often left me feeling like giving up. Sometimes I felt like I just could not handle my trials anymore. Like Mary Ann, the Lord answered my prayers in ways that gave me just enough strength and optimism to get me back on track and able to keep pushing forward.

One day in particular, I remember God answering my prayers in a way I did not expect. I felt especially sick that day, and I was so frustrated, feeling like things would never improve. I had been dealing with my health problems for so long that the pain on bad days made me feel hopeless.

I was in my bed late that morning, praying, and desperately crying for help from my Heavenly Father. I did not think I could survive the pain and misery one more day. In a way, like Mary Ann, I was sitting on the side of the path of life and saying, *I am done. I can't go any farther!*

Like a child, I just wanted someone to make everything better. As immature as this might sound, I thought to myself, *I want my mom.*

I realized there was no way that my mom could be there to help me since she lives in another state, but right away I felt the impression that Luann, my mother in-law, would know I needed her. That gave me great comfort, and I felt peace.

I knew Luann was busy working at the temple that morning and that I just needed to wait until she finished her shift. Sure enough, right after her temple shift was over, she called me to see how I was doing.

I am usually good at holding it together and not showing my emotions, but I started crying over the phone and could barely get out the words to tell her I was not doing well. She told me she would come right over.

She came over, and I was able to express my discouragement with my difficult situation. We talked and talked. It was so nice to have her there to listen, comfort me, and give me the encouragement I needed at that time. I do not know if she realized how much the love she showed me that day helped me. It seems like such a small thing to sit and listen and show empathy, but it was exactly what I needed that day—a mother's love. After her visit, I felt renewed strength and resolve that I could make it through my trials.

Like Mary Ann, my trials were not taken away. Mary Ann still had to face the treacherous path ahead. Similarly, a long road of health struggles lay ahead for me. Like Mary Ann's miraculous pie, my Heavenly Father gave me just what I needed to give me strength to keep going.

Often the Lord sends blessings in unexpected ways. He is aware of our struggles and our needs. When we turn to Him in prayer, He will give us what we need to make it through life's journey. Oftentimes, He does not take our trials away. Instead, He blesses us with *pie*, giving us extra strength and increased capacity to endure, made possible through Christ's Atonement.

He *will* answer our prayers–do not doubt that–but it will be in *His* way. The answers will not always be as obvious as a pie lying in our path or a sweet mother-in-law coming to our rescue, but if we humbly seek, we will find our specific answer and *know* God loves us, for He has promised, "I'll strengthen thee, help thee, and cause thee to stand . . . Upheld by my righteous, omnipotent hand."[2]

17

DEPTH THROUGH SHADOWS

We obtain blessings from our trials that are otherwise unobtainable. Sometimes we do not recognize those blessings when we are in the middle of hardship, but looking back we can see that trials enhanced our life's masterpiece with unique brushstrokes that have given it more depth, purpose, and meaning.

Those brushstrokes are ones that cannot be created without the refining process of adversity. Our paintings need shadows to create dimension and substance. Lessons are learned, we gain Christlike attributes, and our connection with God deepens and flourishes.

I picture a tree being blown in a storm, causing its roots to reach down deep, strengthening its foundation. The root structure becomes more complex and intricate due to hostile winds. Without that strain and pressure, the roots would become shallow and weak. The storm that seems to only wreak havoc, actually increases the tree's capacity to develop and thrive.

A friend of mine told me about an analogy she heard about a surgeon. Imagine an ignorant person looking in on a surgeon in action. The surgeon is cutting open the patient and making the patient bleed. Without understanding what surgery entails, and not knowing there is a greater purpose for surgery and that the result would ultimately benefit and even save the life of the patient, the onlooker might assume the surgeon is malicious.

Does the surgeon not care that the patient is being cut, bleeding, and in pain? Is the surgeon devoid of compassion? From that vantage point, the surgery looks destructive.

In reality, the surgeon knows that the surgery will benefit the patient in the end. The pain is temporary and will be worth the cost. The surgery will be a blessing and will improve the patient's life.

In the same way, our trials that seem to only cause us pain that seem destructive to the life we have envisioned, heal our spirits and make us more Christlike.

James E. Faust said, "The thorns that prick, that stick in the flesh, that hurt, often change lives which seem robbed of significance and hope. This change comes about through a refining process which often seems cruel and hard. In this way the soul can become like soft clay in the hands of the Master in building lives of faith, usefulness, beauty, and strength. For some, the refiner's fire causes a loss of belief and faith in God, but those with eternal perspective understand that such refining is part of the perfection process."[1]

There are blessings hidden within our trials. Sometimes we just need to step back to see the colors of our lives coming together to make us spiritually magnificent.

If you stand up close to a painting and only focus on a small section, the brushstrokes might individually look messy, confusing, and even ugly. Those same brushstrokes, when looked at from a distance, add to the overall beauty and are needed to make the picture complete.

It helps to look at things from a distance, from an eternal perspective, to see the goodness in our lives.

Some blessings come only through shadows of difficulty. Trials stretch us, help us learn and grow, and assist us in developing a stronger relationship with the Savior.

It is easy to focus on the messy strokes and to be blind to the overall composition that God is creating.

My blessings came in surprising ways. For many years I could not achieve worldly success, but I do believe I created a happy place for our children to be, and God changed me in the process.

Also, looking back I can now see that my health trial also added beneficial brushstrokes to our children's masterpieces. In my imperfect state, I was the mother my children needed. From living in an imperfect household where everyone had to pitch in and help each other, they became compassionate, loving, and independent individuals.

For example, one Christmas, when I was in the midst of the worst of my health problems, Sierra, who was only about eight or nine years old at the time, was sitting at the counter making her Christmas list to Santa.

I decided to go check it out. I came up behind her and started reading her Christmas list. She had quite the long list of toys and electronics, but at the very end of her list of the things she wanted for Christmas, she had written, "And if possible, above all, my mom's health."

I was overcome with emotion knowing that such a young child would make me and my well-being a priority over those worldly items that she desired so much. My eyes filled with tears, amazed at the unselfish, Christlike love of a child.

So many moments like these have helped me see that my

health trials helped our children become who they are today. The perfect mother I had envisioned being, that I thought they were missing out on, would not have helped their growth as individuals. My many inabilities helped them to grow and develop, becoming both capable and Christlike. When I wanted to be the one serving them, they stepped in and served me.

I have memories of Spencer stepping in to help me at church. My arms always seemed full of diaper bags and church bags, making it difficult to keep five kids reigned in. Tyson had to be at church early for meetings and other obligations, so it was up to me to get the kids there and back home. I remember feeling like a juggling sideshow on the way into and out of church.

When little Spencer would offer to carry one of my bags for me, I felt such relief. I was amazed that a child so young would think to offer assistance; kids that age are usually oblivious to adults needing help. Such a small gesture made a huge difference in my life. Having one less thing to worry about lifted a literal weight off my shoulder. He eased my burdens with his kindness, and I was able to walk with a greater calmness and composure. I made sure to express my immense gratitude to him, and he learned the value of Christlike service.

All our children learned an awareness of the needs of others because of my illness. They would often amaze me with their compassion. So many times, they would come up to me when I was lying on the couch or on my bed and ask me how I was feeling. That gesture in and of itself touched me. I do not remember being aware of my parents' needs or feelings when I was young. Like many children, I thought the world revolved around me. I have learned from our kids what it means to be Christlike.

Not only did our children ask me how I was feeling, but they also offered to serve me when I told them I did not feel well. I remember each of them, many times over the years, asking me if I wanted a drink or food. There were so many instances when that was exactly what I needed, so one of them would bring me a drink of water or something simple to eat like a grilled cheese or peanut butter sandwich. I do not think they realized what a blessing that was in my life at the time. Oftentimes, I would be lying there so hungry or thirsty, but I did not have the energy or willpower to get up to do anything about it. They were my angels who lightened my burdens.

Sometimes they went above and beyond, making a game out of bringing me food. They wrote out a menu of options as if they were working at a restaurant. For example, the main course options would be something like macaroni and cheese, grilled cheese, or a quesadilla. The side options would be something like apple slices, baby carrots, or yogurt. They would bring me the menu along with a pen and have me check or circle the items of my choice. Then they would go to meticulous lengths to bring me the desired items laid out on a plate in an attractive way. I felt so special to have so many little hands trying so hard to make my life easier.

My trial gave our children the opportunity to see others' needs and to serve. They also learned gratitude. Because I did not have the energy to take care of all their needs, they had to pitch in and help themselves and each other. Fulfilling those needs themselves helped them pay attention to and acknowledge those who assisted and served them. They did not take for granted the things people did to make their lives easier and better.

I noticed that when I did have the energy to make dinner, the children would pour out words of gratitude such as,

"Thank you so much for the delicious dinner, Mom." They showed that same gratitude when I had the energy to help them with other tasks as well. They were extra grateful for the things I did for them because I was not always able to do so.

They were also full of gratitude when one of their siblings or their dad did something for them, such as making a meal. One reason for their abundant gratitude was that they knew by experience the work it took to make those meals and to provide certain services because they often had to perform those tasks themselves. They knew first-hand that meals took time, effort, and sacrifice. When everything is handed to children on a silver platter, rather than feeling grateful, they tend to expect it and feel entitled to that service on their behalf.

It was eye-opening to me when I realized the shadows in my painting were building our children's character. I wanted so badly to be a mother who took care of all their needs, but it seemed more beneficial to their spiritual growth and independence when I could not do that. They matured and flourished when they were given more responsibilities and when they were expected to contribute to the well-being of the family.

I learned that children gain a positive self-esteem by being productive and doing things for themselves. Our society often tries to increase children's self-esteem by showering them with praise, telling them how amazing they are.

In contrast to empty praise, kids take approval to heart if it is for something they have accomplished. Although kids appreciate compliments, through their own performance and achievement of tasks, their confidence grows regardless of praise. Children feel positive about themselves when they feel capable. They gain confidence and self-respect when they learn skills that demonstrate their independence, knowledge, and abilities, rather than just being told they are great.

Our children, rather than feeling that life was unfair because they had to do many things for themselves, gained a sense of pride in knowing how to accomplish various tasks. I saw their confidence increase the more they were asked to do. Learning how to work hard and to contribute to the welfare of the family brought contentment and happiness.

That does not mean that our children never complained about working. Yet, one interesting phenomenon I learned is that the more children consistently work, the less they whine. I often reminded our children of that fact. Whenever they complained about jobs assigned to them, I told them, "I have learned that children who whine about doing jobs, do not work enough. It sounds like you need more work to do."

That quickly stopped the grumbling. I did find it to be true that the more our children worked, the less they murmured because working became a commonplace occurrence that was expected. It became a part of everyday life. Learning how to contribute to the organization and cleanliness of the home helped our children become hard-working and well-adjusted.

I hope others do not read about the blessings my family and I experienced during my trials and start to compare. Our trials and blessings are ones that our family specifically needed.

God orchestrates our lives in a way that most effectively leads us back to Him. He will bestow blessings that cater to our individual spiritual needs. He uses our individual hardships to bless us and change our Spirits in a way that is most beneficial for us. We can rest assured that He will help us rise above our circumstances.

He will create beauty out of the shadows of our lives.

18

ANGELIC LUSTER

When we were told that it was time for Tyson to be released from his calling in our ward's bishopric, a stake presidency member asked if we would both share our testimonies in church that Sunday. We both agreed to the request.

That Sunday morning, I woke up with a flare in my symptoms. My body hurt, and the fatigue was debilitating. In tears, I told Tyson that I did not think I could make it to church to bear my testimony. He asked if I wanted a priesthood blessing. I said that I did, so he called our home teacher to come help with the blessing.

I do not remember much about the blessing except the words, *Angels will be there to bear you up*. The blessing ended, and I knew I would be able to go to church that day. Sure enough, I had the energy to get ready and go to church.

When the time came for me to bear my testimony, I walked up to the pulpit with strength, and I bore my testimony of the blessings our family had received from the Lord through Tyson's service. It felt like an out-of-body experience. The Spirit around me was palpable, and I was able to share what was in my heart with ease. I did not feel or see angels around me, but I felt the power of the Holy Ghost so strongly that I knew they helped me that day.

Doctrine and Covenants 84:88 says, "I will be on your right hand and on your left, and my Spirit shall be in your hearts, and mine angels round about you, to bear you up."

Another experience happened in the middle of a bad night. I was so miserable and could not sleep, so I went into the living room so I would not wake Tyson. I felt so sick and helpless. Once again, I just wanted a break from my problems. I knelt by the couch and pleaded with Heavenly Father. I was so congested and in pain. Feeling at the end of my rope, I asked a question that showed my lack of faith. I asked, *why? Why do I have to suffer so much?*

I felt the Spirit answer in a way I did not expect. I had the thought; *your children need the angels right now that are there to help you.* Then I felt the Spirit draw my attention to the wall behind me.

For the past couple of years, I had been teaching the children about their ancestors and hanging pictures of those ancestors on that wall one at a time. I wanted the children to learn about the faithful lives of their ancestors because great spiritual strength comes from knowing the stories of progenitors. Because we had learned about so many ancestors, our wall was covered with their pictures.

I was overwhelmed with peace as I realized the Spirit was telling me that some of those ancestors were angels for our family during my difficulties. I was a little confused because our children did not seem to have any specific problems or needs that I knew of. I could not figure out why they needed angels at that time, and I still do not know the exact purpose. I also do not know of any specific experiences where our children felt the presence of those angels, but the Spirit told me that angels were there in my time of need and that our children needed their influence.

I realized that my prayers during my time of sickness were more frequent, earnest, and sincere than ever before. I wondered if angels are sent to add luster to our paintings at times when our prayers are most fervent. I also wondered if in my past, on days that I had felt abandoned by the Lord, there were actually angels helping me and my family in ways that I could not see. I love the thought that our ancestors can be our angels when we plead for help.

Many times, my angels were the people in my life.

Jeffrey R. Holland said, "When we speak of those who are instruments in the hand of God, we are reminded that not all angels are from the other side of the veil."[1]

I already mentioned how our children were my ministering angels. They served and blessed me often with their love.

Tyson was also an angel in my life, a constant rock that I could always lean on. His optimism, fortitude, and service blessed my life greatly as he made up for my lack of vitality. Although I felt bad that I was not able to be the fun mom I wanted to be, it was so nice that Tyson stepped in and more than made up for what I lacked by being a fun dad.

Despite my health struggles, our children had an amazing childhood full of fun trips and adventures because of Tyson. He taught them how to ski, mountain bike, rock climb, and ride motorcycles. I love that he also patiently taught me those things as well. I often doubted that my low energy levels would allow me to participate, but with his encouragement, his fun plans got me out of the house and got my adrenaline going, which increased my energy more than I thought possible.

Tyson also made up for my deficiencies by demonstrating to the children how to be a hard worker. I should not have worried about the fact that our children were not learning that pattern from me. They had the perfect example to follow with Tyson as their dad. He worked long and hard at the dental office, and when he was not at the office, he diligently fulfilled his duties at home and church. The children saw the joy Tyson found in serving everyone around him, and they wanted to be like him.

Tyson's love for home-improvement projects was also infectious. His positive example especially benefited our children when he included them in those projects. They loved taking part and feeling useful, and they learned that satisfaction comes from a job well-done.

For example, I have a fond memory of all our young kids outside helping Tyson plant flowers in the flower beds. Smiles spread widely across their faces as they took turns transporting flowers to their dad so he could place them in the ground. They loved taking part and being helpful. He taught them to work hard and often. They found deep gratification in learning valuable skills at his side. He was definitely an angel in my life as he brought joy, excitement, strength, and energy into my life and the lives of our children.

My in-laws were also angels in my life. Delmar and Luann were always there for me when I needed them. They served me and my family in so many ways. I learned through them that food is a meaningful way to transmit love. Each of them lightened my load and made me feel loved because of the various meals they made for our family. From the countless fancy dinners during large family gatherings at their house, to personal deliveries of hot soup and bread to our house, I felt their love deeply, and they repeatedly brightened difficult days.

For a while, Delmar served his children who lived locally by bringing each family dinner once a week. I always got excited when Delmar called and said, "I'm bringing dinner tonight. I will drop it off around 6:00." During that time period, he humorously gave himself the nickname Chef-Boy-R-Delmar.

Sometimes he brought homemade casseroles or soups, and other times he brought takeout from local restaurants. I told him each time what a blessing those meals were in my life. When I knew a meal was being delivered, I felt such relief in knowing I did not need to muster up the energy to prepare food for our family. Because that task was taken off my list for the day, I was often able to use my limited energy to accomplish other jobs around the house.

Although my own parents and siblings lived too far away to be of immediate assistance, they were still my angels. I always knew they would drop everything to come help me if I asked them to, and they shared their love with me by praying on my behalf.

At one time, they decided to hold a special fast and to pray for me. I felt especially blessed with strength during that month. I sent an email to my family to thank everyone for the month of prayers.

I was so touched when my dad replied, "You're welcome, but I hope you know that you are always in our prayers, not just this month."

Their continuous love gave me strength to endure. They were also the examples I looked up to in how to face life with faith and optimism. During trials of their own, they demonstrated how to faithfully keep covenants and devotedly follow God's will despite hardship.

So many friends were also angels in my life because of the love and concern they showed me. I did not often share with them that I was struggling, so I know they would have appreciated me letting them into my life more, but it was just so comforting to know that they were available if I needed them. They stepped in whenever they knew there was a need to fill.

When one friend of mine offered to help clean my house, I learned a lesson about letting people serve me. My first thought when she offered was that I did not want her cleaning up our messes. Also, realizing she had a busy life of her own, I did not want to add to her load. I almost talked myself out of letting her help, but then I had the thought, *You have been praying so hard for help. Why wouldn't you let God answer your prayer through your friend?*

That hit me hard. It seemed silly to pray for help but then refuse the help that was offered by one of God's ministering angels. I decided I needed to be better at letting people serve me.

I learned another lesson about service from that experience. My friend demonstrated a great method of offering service that I hope to emulate. It was easier to accept her service because she gave me a few options to choose from, and then she asked which service would be of most benefit to me.

One idea she gave me was to come clean my house on a day I was not feeling well. That option was difficult for me to accept because I felt weird about someone working so hard around me while I lay there watching and feeling lazy.

Another option she gave me was to come help me catch up on cleaning on a day that I felt well. I loved that idea! It was a way she could help me that would not leave me feeling awkward.

I felt much more comfortable accepting her service knowing I could be there working alongside her. I loved that she listened to my feedback rather than just serving me in a way that she assumed was best.

Not long after her offer, I woke up one morning with more energy than normal, and I realized I had the energy to clean the house. It still was not easy to call my friend for help, but I felt so much better about it because I would not have to just watch her clean. It also helped me to remember the prompting I had earlier to *let God answer my prayers through His earthly angels*.

My friend came over that morning after I called her, and we accomplished so much more than I could have on my own. It was amazing to have an angel there to help me.

One of the greatest services my earthly angels gave me was the gift of a listening ear. There was not a lot that people could do to solve my problems; they could not take away my misery or my pain, but they could listen and offer sympathy. When loved ones truly listened and sought to understand, my burdens felt much lighter. I did not need them to fix my circumstances, I just needed them to offer compassion.

For example, one time I went to visit a childhood friend whom I had not seen for a long time. We sat on her porch and caught up on everything that had been happening in our lives. When I told her about my health struggles, she listened, asked questions, and listened some more.

At one point in the conversation, my friend started to cry because it made her so sad that I had to go through such a difficult trial. Her empathy touched my heart so deeply, more than any other act of service could have. In seeking to understand what I was going through, she gained compassion for my pain and showed pure charity. Through her, I felt God's love.

"Indeed heaven never seems closer than when we see the love of God manifested in the kindness and devotion of people so good and so pure that *angelic* is the only word that comes to mind."[2]

I am so grateful for all the earthly angels in my life. My artwork would not be the same without the stunning luster so many people added to the overall effect of my painting. I hope that I can learn from their examples and find ways to serve and bless those around me. I want others to feel God's love through me.

19

ARTISTIC INTERPRETATION

One day I had an extreme allergic reaction to Ibuprofen. The reaction caused severe stomach pain, and my asthma went out of control. Although it was a horrible episode, I felt gratitude because it became a key to unlocking my diagnosis.

When my doctor heard about the incident, he connected the dots of my symptoms and diagnosed me with Aspirin Exacerbated Respiratory Disease (AERD). Finally, someone was able to interpret my confusing painting. Finally, everything made sense.

AERD is a respiratory disease that used to be referred to as Samter's Triad because it manifests in a triad of symptoms– chronic asthma, sinusitis with nasal polyps, and an allergy to NSAIDS (nonsteroidal anti-inflammatory drugs which include Aspirin and Ibuprofen). Those with AERD also struggle with chronic fatigue because their bodies are constantly fighting chronic inflammation. Symptoms can also include loss of sense of smell and chronic hives.

I was so excited to have a name for my condition! After

years of dealing with confusing symptoms, I felt validated in knowing what was wrong with my body. Although the doctor did not know of an easy fix for the disease, my hope for a brighter future increased. I loved that I would finally be able to tell people what was wrong with me, rather than just saying that I felt sick.

The doctor decided to refer me to an ENT (Ear, Nose, & Throat specialist). Part of me was hopeful; I finally had some direction. The other part of me was skeptical after previously being told by a sinus specialist that I was a lost cause.

Fortunately, the new ENT was more optimistic about being able to improve my condition. With my sinuses full of chronically infected tissue, he saw sinus surgery as an opportunity to give my body a fresh start. Although he could not guarantee it would be a long-term cure, he assured me that emptying out my sinuses could only improve my health. It made sense that being able to breathe through my nose again would benefit me.

The sinus surgery went well, and I experienced a quick recovery. It felt so nice to be able to breathe out of my nose again. In addition, I got my asthma under control with a daily preventer inhaler. My quality of life improved overall, but I was discouraged that some symptoms remained. I had hoped the surgery would increase my energy level and that my sinus pain would subside, but that was not the case. I went back to the ENT for a follow-up appointment and told him about the symptoms that lingered. He suggested a revisionary surgery to clear out my sinuses even more.

The second surgery was minor because the first surgery had already cleared out my sinuses so well. My sinuses healed quickly, but I still did not notice improvement in my energy levels or pain. When I told the ENT about my stubborn symptoms, he did not have much else to recommend.

He prescribed a nasal spray to help, and he casually mentioned that I might want to investigate aspirin desensitization as a possible treatment option.

I left the ENT office with aspirin desensitization on my mind. I had never heard of it before. The way he mentioned it in passing, I did not think it could possibly be a treatment with potential. I assumed he would have been more enthusiastic about it had it been a probable remedy. Since he did not seem to know much about the treatment, I decided to research it myself. I was open to anything that might improve my health.

My research revealed that aspirin desensitization is a common procedure used to treat AERD. The treatment helps those with the disease to be able to take aspirin and other NSAIDs without having an allergic reaction. That part made sense. The confusing result of the procedure is that it also tends to improve all the other symptoms of the disease. It is such a strange phenomenon that a disease that makes people allergic to aspirin can be treated effectively with aspirin.

For the procedure, "you're challenged with graded doses of aspirin.... Your provider starts by giving a very small dose of aspirin and watches to see if you react. When you get to the dose that causes symptoms, you'll keep getting that dose until you can tolerate this dose without adverse reaction. You'll then get higher and higher doses of the drug. As you keep getting the higher doses, your body will start to accept the drug without reacting."[1]

The downside of the treatment is that for the tolerance to aspirin to be maintained and for relief of symptoms to persist, aspirin must be taken every day afterward. Even skipping a few days of taking aspirin will revert patients back to their original state of being allergic to NSAIDs. In that case, the other symptoms of the disease also return to their prior magnitude.

Since the procedure was not widely practiced at the time of my research, the closest clinic that offered the treatment was in California, a couple of states away from my home in Idaho. When I called the clinic, hoping to schedule the procedure, I learned that the timing of my call could not have been more perfect.

She told me that the most effective time to have the treatment done is five months after sinus surgery. That timing is best because the sinuses have just enough time to heal from the surgery before the polyps start growing again. Starting the therapy in that time frame can slow or even stop the polyps from developing.

When she checked the clinic's schedule, I was amazed to hear that the next available appointment was five months from the date of my recent surgery. It seemed too perfect to be a coincidence. I felt the Lord guiding my life.

When the date arrived for my appointment, I got on an airplane to fly to San Diego. I distinctly remember that flight. I sat in a window seat looking out as the plane flew through the clouds. I felt a strong impression that I was being carried in the palms of the Lord's hands. I felt a burning sensation in my soul. I knew that feeling was from the Spirit, revealing to me that Heavenly Father had led me to that moment. He led me to discover that treatment for my disease at just the right time in my life. Because of Him, I was on my way to improved health.

The aspirin desensitization was not a perfect cure, but it did improve my symptoms and my way of life. It reduced the inflammation in my body which in turn helped my overall health. Aspirin therapy decreased the speed of the growth of the sinus polyps, and it decreased my asthma symptoms. I continued to experience quite a bit of fatigue and sinus pain still, but I was so grateful for the strides my body made.

The aspirin desensitization decreased my symptoms for a couple of years, and I know it was an answer to my prayers to ease my suffering during that time.

For an unknown reason, my body started having allergic reactions to the aspirin again. With those episodes happening frequently, I felt like it was time to stop the treatment, and the doctor agreed.

Looking back, I can now see that everything seemed to line up so perfectly. By the time I stopped the aspirin therapy, new medications had come out that were proven to improve the symptoms of AERD. I was able to seamlessly switch from aspirin therapy over to a new biologic medication in a timely manner, not leaving time in between for sinus polyps to grow back.

My experience with the new medication was like my experience with aspirin desensitization because it decreased my symptoms enough that I could function better, but it was not a cure-all. By the time I felt like its effectiveness was wearing off after a year or so, another new medication was available for me to try.

Each time I stopped a treatment, a new medication came out at just the right time for me, and each medication helped a little better than the previous one. I felt so blessed to always be on top of the latest medical breakthroughs.

I joined an AERD Facebook group, and through that I learned about a new medication that showed great promise for treating the disease. I even found out about it before my doctor did. At my next appointment, I asked the doctor if I could try the new medication, and he said he would get back to me because the drug representative was coming to teach them about it later that day. I ended up being among the first

AERD patients to try the newest and best medication for the disease. The blessings just kept pouring down.

That medication changed my life. I quickly started to feel better than I had in the past thirteen years. I realized that prayers about health problems can be answered through medical advancements and treatments. Great peace came when I found out about a doctor who devoted her life to leading the research of AERD and possible remedies, and she continues to do so today. I wondered if the prayers from me, my family, and others with the disease, helped those researching the disease to be guided by the Spirit in finding remedies.

I am currently still taking that medication for AERD, and it has been an amazing blessing in my life. I have been able to do so much more than I used to. I still struggle with low energy and pain, but it is much more manageable now, and I can push through it easier. It has been such a blessing to have more energy to clean the house and to cook meals for my family. I also find great joy in exercising more. When I get to participate in sports and outdoor activities with friends and family, my heart feels like it will burst with joy.

The trials I have been through have made the good moments of life so much sweeter. For example, when I have the energy to clean the house, I am filled with happiness and satisfaction. It feels so good to be able to work hard and accomplish tasks. I do not take my abilities and stamina for granted.

20

ADDING DIMENSION

After all I have been through and all that God has taught me through my struggles, I wish I could say that I always have a positive attitude now. It was hard to write this book without feeling like a hypocrite because I do not always practice what I preach. It is hard to keep my will aligned with God's and to stay at peace with my situation.

Yes, my health is better than it has been for years, but my body still gets in the way of being as productive as I would like. I accomplish more than I used to, but I must push through fatigue and pain to do those things. My life is easier, but when frequent pain and fatigue still loom over me, although to a lesser degree, I often drift back into a negative mindset and get discouraged.

I realize how ungrateful that must sound after receiving so many answers to prayer, but chronic illness is difficult. When bumpy roads are extremely long, it is hard not to yearn to find an easier and more fulfilling route.

Some trials seem relentless. In those times, it helps to remember that the goal is to endure to the end. It is okay to feel sadness and discouragement. What is important is to keep pressing forward, taking one step in front of the other, taking one day at a time. Slowly, you will see God adding dimension to your artwork.

Sometimes I get overwhelmed when I think of a lifetime of chronic illness, so it helps to instead focus on making the best of the day directly ahead of me. Realizing the Master Painter is in control, and letting Him have that control, brings contentment and peace.

We will stumble at times along the path, but it is not important that we not fall; in fact, it is expected. What is important is that we get back up. We should reach out to God to help us get up when it is beyond our own strength to do so. The falls tighten our bond with God when we do that.

Trials that are lengthy and difficult require a lot of faith and prayer to endure. I find myself in constant need of the Lord's guiding light and enabling power in my life. While it helps to take one day at a time, it also helps to see things from an eternal perspective. I often have a hard time seeing past the storms of life that immediately surround me.

Hope and courage come when I try to look at things through God's vantage point and the grand scheme of things. Prayer, scripture study, and temple attendance will keep our sights set on eternal goals. Doing those things helps us remember that our mortal life has a greater purpose.

This life is but a moment—it is a speck on the line of eternity. It is a brief sojourn where we are tested and refined so we can one day return to live with the Father and the Son. We are promised blessings beyond measure if we keep our covenants and endure to the end. If we keep hold of the iron rod, nothing will deter us from reaching our eternal destination.

When Joseph Smith faced extreme difficulties, the Lord advised, "Hold on thy way."[1]

God's plan is a plan of happiness. If we are faithful during the storms of life, we will receive the greatest gift God can offer His sons and daughters, Celestial glory.

I have found that when I hold fast to God's promises, He gives me glimpses into eternity. Those heavenly reminders motivate me to keep moving forward. It can be frustrating, though, when those glimpses do not come frequently or when I am asking for them.

When I went to the temple during my most difficult years, I prayed and hoped for spiritual enlightenment. I thought that faithfully serving in God's house would qualify me for spiritual experiences. I learned that I needed to obey God's commandments consistently over and over, and then He would bless me on His timetable.

Maybe others have spiritual experiences frequently, but in my life, I have had to hold on to the iron rod for long durations before God demonstrates His power in obvious ways. When I stay on His path and have faith in Him even when spiritual experiences are not abundant, He blesses me for my dedication when He sees fit.

After going to the temple many times when I was miserable and desperate for heavenly inspiration, my most powerful spiritual experience came when I was not looking for it. Tyson and I went to the temple on a day when my trials were not at the forefront. Unlike other times when I felt at a tipping point emotionally and was seeking wholeheartedly to feel the Spirit speak to me, I sat in the temple without anything on my mind. Although my trials were still difficult, I was not emotional about it. It was one of those days when I was just going through the motions.

In the temple, out of nowhere, the most intense flood of

the Spirit engulfed me. The feeling came on so suddenly and forcefully that my body reacted with an immediate gush of tears. The feeling was so overwhelming that I felt like I had entered God's presence. The sudden emotions would have made sense if I were emotionally sensitive that day, but I went from stoic to intense sobbing in a matter of seconds. Tyson was probably embarrassed to be with me because the tears were uncontrollable. I tried to keep quiet because the temple is a place of reverence, but I could not. I struggled to control the sobs. The feeling was so intense that I wondered if something as miraculous as a healing had just occurred. I secretly hoped that was the case.

The tears gradually subsided, and I was left in awe at the experience. I had not been praying for help or feeling in particular need, yet God blessed me to feel His spirit stronger than I ever had before.

It did not take long to realize that I had not been healed of my disease; rather, it was an experience in which God helped me feel that He was indeed aware of me and my struggles. After enduring for so long and consistently keeping my covenants, He gave me that brief glimpse into eternity. He displayed His power and love at a time I did not expect, according to His timetable.

That experience taught me that through long suffering and enduring to the end, I can count on His blessings. I can have faith that He is adding dimension to my painting. Sometimes the blessings come immediately, and sometimes they come after continually holding onto the iron rod on a tiresome, long, and bumpy road. We need to keep going to church and to the temple even during times when it feels like we are just going through the motions.

Consistent spiritual commitment brings heavenly support and strength, although not always perceptible. My short spiritual experience is nothing compared to the glorious blessing of exaltation that God has prepared for those who faithfully endure to the end.

> "Wherefore, ye must press forward with a steadfastness in Christ, having a perfect brightness of hope, and a love of God and of all men. Wherefore, if ye shall press forward, feasting upon the word of Christ, and endure to the end, behold, thus saith the Father: Ye shall have eternal life."[2]

21

HIS MASTERPIECE

*E*veryone faces trials, and we all suffer in different ways. Some mourn the loss of loved ones, some face debilitating depression and/or anxiety, and some struggle with the chains of addiction. Some face the heartache of infertility, some deal with psychological consequences of abuse, and some suffer from loneliness. Some face financial hardship, some wrestle with same-sex attraction, and some deal with the emotional pain of watching loved ones stray from God's path. The list could go on and on. There are so many different struggles that people face.

Life is hard, but it is also beautiful.

My heart aches when I think of all the suffering of people around me. Even those who externally seem to have perfect lives, have difficult struggles or have layers to their paintings that are not seen from the outside. That realization makes me determined to treat everyone with greater compassion and less judgment. We would all benefit from more kindness and love.

I find great peace in knowing that the Master Painter is in

control and is aware of each of us. Although we have to wait at times for His assistance, His artistic techniques enhance our spiritual strength and help us reach our divine potential.

He lets us experience hardship because He knows we need shadows in our paintings to add depth to our souls. It pains Him to see us suffer, but He knows that our trials can turn us to Him and help us obtain His grace. When we humbly seek access to the Savior's perfect palette, He will heal our spirits, aid us in overcoming the natural man, and help us become more Christlike.

One of my favorite Bible stories is about a woman who suffered from an issue of blood for twelve years. Having so much faith that the Savior could cure her of her disease, she made her way to Him. She found Him in a crowd, and without Him seeing her, she reached out and touched His robe. She was immediately healed.

"And Jesus said, Somebody hath touched me: for I perceive that virtue is gone out of me."[1] He then said to her, "Daughter, be of good comfort: thy faith hath made thee whole."[2]

I love that story and have yearned to have a similar experience of healing. I have often put myself in the woman's shoes and imagined how glorious it would be to stand so near to the Savior that I could be healed by merely reaching out to Him.

I get choked up when I imagine how incredible it would be to instantly have relief from all the symptoms I have suffered for so many years. To have the intense weight of my burdens lifted from my weak body would indeed be miraculous and life changing. I imagine the overpowering feeling of gratitude that would overflow from my heart. I would feel totally indebted to my Savior and willing to do anything to show my appreciation.

Jeffrey R. Holland taught, "Another word for *virtue* is *power*. When the woman came to touch the hem of Christ's garment, in the scene in the New Testament, He said, 'Virtue [has] gone out of me' (Luke 8:46). The original Greek New Testament language for that is *power*."[3]

Knowing that virtue means power adds even greater meaning to the story for me. The woman received the Savior's power (virtue) when she reached out to Him in faith.

In my life, although it might not be God's will for me to be physically healed, I want to follow the woman's example and faithfully reach out to the Savior in faith to receive His spiritual power. If I seek access to His superior palette through prayer and covenant keeping, He can impart His virtue on me. Through His grace, I can be freed of spiritual weakness, which is just as miraculous as physical healing, yet eternally more significant.

Just as freeing as it would be to have physical symptoms of disease lifted from the body, the grace of Jesus Christ frees us from spiritual disease. He heals our spirits by bestowing His spiritual gifts on us, which "greatly [enlarges] the soul."[4]

I am so grateful for the compensating power made available through the Atonement of Jesus Christ. No matter how weak we are, the Savior can fill in the colors we lack. In fact, like the woman in the story, weakness and trial can humble us and initiate our desire to seek out and reach for His grace.

Hard times become the catalyst for spiritual refinement, giving God the opportunity to create a magnificent masterpiece of our lives.

I assumed my life would be easy and that I could color inside the lines and get the expected results. With a worthwhile design in mind and amazing artistic influences to follow, I knew I could create the work of art I yearned for.

Little did I know, the Master Painter had a more advantageous method in mind. He knew better techniques to help me produce a more spectacular creation than I had envisioned.

Although part of that process involved acquiring undesirable hues that I would not have chosen myself, the Master Painter used those tones to improve my painting and the painting of my family. I am full of gratitude for the way the Savior continually bestowed His power on me during hardship, helping me become more like Him.

During my most difficult times of trial, I stood so close to my life's painting that I could only see the darkest shades and the messiest brushstrokes. It was hard to understand why God would let such ugly tones infiltrate my canvas. The bleeding colors not only seemed pointless but detrimental.

Now that I have stepped back, I see the opposite is true. Times of darkness and shadows were essential in generating an artwork full of depth and meaning–an exquisite composition. My trials blessed me in ways otherwise impossible. Through the grace of Jesus Christ, He enabled me to acquire His divine attributes, making my artwork glorious and divine.

I savor the sweetness of life more intensely after tasting the bitter.

Neal A. Maxwell taught, "The cavity which suffering carves into our souls will one day also be the receptacle of joy."[5]

I love that visual. I have experienced that joy because of my trials. Through the grace of Jesus Christ, the cavity that has been carved into my soul has been filled with spiritual strength.

L. Todd Budge quoted a 13th-century poet:

"Sorrow prepares you for joy. It violently sweeps

everything out of your house, so that new joy can find space to enter. It shakes the yellow leaves from the bough of your heart, so that fresh, green leaves can grow in their place. It pulls up the rotten roots, so that new roots hidden beneath have room to grow. Whatever sorrow shakes from your heart, far better things will take their place."[6]

I do not know what future brushstrokes and colors will be added to my artwork. I do not know how long my current medication will continue to help. I do not know what obstacles I will face down the road, due to my disease. I do not know if my health problems will become the least of my worries in the future as I face even more difficult trials.

What I *do* know is that by following the eternal rules of composition through faith, prayer, and covenant keeping, the grace of Jesus Christ made available through His Atonement, will give me strength to endure the moments of uncontrollable, bleeding colors.

I have faith in God's divine process because I know He gives me just enough paint at just the right times. I find great comfort in knowing that any of His design adjustments will be for my ultimate improvement, helping me become more like my Savior.

By savoring the creative process and submitting my will to God's, the brushstrokes of my life will come together according to God's design. Through the grace of Jesus Christ, I will become a magnificent masterpiece in His hands.

Joy will find place in my heart, and beauty will continue to emerge because, "I can do all things through Christ which strengtheneth me."[7]

AFTERWORD

Life's Miracles

This book is one of my life's miracles. I saw God's hand so clearly throughout the process, reminding me that He is in the details. Writing this book with His help has confirmed to me that when God gives me a prompting that seems unfeasible, I need to have faith that He will make the impossible possible. Looking back, I can see all the small miracles that came together to create this big miracle.

The first small miracle occurred years ago during the worst of my health struggles. I went to a church women's conference, and the talks touched me so deeply, giving me an added measure of spiritual strength. I felt buoyed up and ready to face my trials with faith in my Savior. Toward the end of the conference, I had an unexpected thought which I now know was a spiritual prompting.

I thought, *I want to give a talk at one of these conferences someday so I can give that same spiritual upliftment to others.*

That thought shocked me. I have always had a major fear of public speaking, so feeling that desire slip into my heart and mind was unexpected. I can see now that God gave me a glimpse into my future so that I could prepare myself mentally and emotionally.

Because of that spiritual prompting, I was not surprised when I was asked years later to speak at a women's conference. I knew it was something that God wanted me to do, and remarkably, it was something I desired to do as well. It was a miracle that not only was I not stressed about being the main speaker at the event, but I felt peace and excitement in knowing it was something God had prepared me for.

Writing the talk was an incredible spiritual experience because of the enormous amount of help I received from the Spirit. Although I was blessed to have many thoughts, lessons, and talks I had written at other times in my life about trials to use as groundwork, I wondered how I could possibly combine all the ideas and map them out on paper in a way that would make sense and flow in a way that would make an impact on people. I know I had heavenly help in both the ideas and the organization of the talk.

I remember at times thinking about my talk as I was going about my day, and the Spirit helped me think of wording to explain experiences and analogies in a coherent way. I also remember lying in bed, trying to figure out how to connect certain parts of my talk in a way that made sense. It was like I could see the different fragments that didn't fit well together, and then the Spirit helped me move those fragments around in my head until it flowed in a most impactful way.

The Spirit even gave me a strong feeling of peace afterward, confirming to me that it was not my own skills and abilities that made my thoughts and ideas come together beautifully.

It felt amazing to be an instrument in the Lord's hands. I knew the words I was writing were ones He wanted His children to hear, to buoy them up in their difficulties. He was directing me.

After the conference, I immediately got the feeling that I needed to give that talk to more audiences. I was not about to advertise my talk to other groups, so I waited and wondered if God would direct me to others who needed the message.

Not long after, I was asked to present my talk at two other events. I was not surprised or scared when I was asked to give my talk again because the Spirit had made it known earlier that I needed to share it again. It was providence. I knew it was something I was meant to do with my life. Although I still got stage fright, I was so grateful for the opportunity because it gave an extra purpose to my trials. My trials became a means for me to uplift others and to teach about the Atonement of Jesus Christ.

Each time I presented my talk, people from all walks of life told me the message was just what they needed to hear. After seeing that my talk was beneficial to so many, I started getting a new impression. *Could I write a book based on my talk?*

As quickly as that thought entered my mind, doubts crept in. I had no idea how to write a book. I never considered myself a writer. I had written a couple of short blog posts in the past about trials for my friend's inspirational blog, but that was all I had written besides school papers. I also did not know if I had enough things to say to fill a whole book. It sounded so complicated. I did not know where to start.

My biggest hesitancy came from the fear of exposing my personal life and feelings in a book. It scared me to think of people reading about my personal struggles and spiritual experiences that were so dear to me. I worried I would be judged harshly and my spiritual experiences would be minimized. Therefore, assuming my initial desire to write a book was just my own random thought, I pushed the idea aside.

When the thought came back, I pushed it aside. It came back again, and I pushed it aside again. Although I had the thought multiple times, it came intermittently, spread over a long period of time. I started to notice that the times the thought would come to me were times when I was thinking about what God wanted me to do with my life. I started to feel like it was part of God's plan for me.

Eventually, I started to feel like I was ignoring God's promptings and that I needed to try. What was the worst that could happen? I decided to just start writing and see what happened from there.

Another miracle was God putting the right people in my path to help me with the writing process. I know it was not an accident that the first person I decided to tell about my attempt to write a book was my friend Charissa Stastny. Since she is an accomplished author, I decided to tell her about my undertaking. Up until that point, I had kept it to myself in fear of failure. I did not want anyone to know I had tried and failed.

Telling Charissa ended up being a launchpad for my success. She offered to read through the chapters I was working on and provide feedback and editing suggestions. Her kindness touched me and motivated me to get my writing organized so I could send her something resembling finished chapters.

I believe it was part of God's plan to have Charissa involved in my writing. She became an integral part of the process. When I sent her the first couple chapters, she offered much-needed constructive criticism. As I followed her advice and trusted in her expertise, the book started to take shape. My confidence increased as I applied her suggestions. Her technical skill and her advice about content enhanced my writing every step of the way. Her constant encouragement and optimism built me up during times of doubt and discouragement. She always knew the right thing to say, inspiring me to keep moving forward. She helped me believe in myself. I am so glad God placed her in my path. I will always be grateful to her for the many hours of effort she devoted to helping me succeed.

I also do not think it was by chance that I got help from Macayle Stucki. I had never met Macayle, but one day, her cousin who is a good friend of mine, shared her Instagram post about trials. I read the post and immediately knew I wanted to include her thoughts in my book. I was so excited when I sent her a message and she not only gave me permission to include her thoughts, but she also told me of her enthusiasm for my book's subject matter because of her expertise in helping people with mental health.

I decided it would be good for someone with her expertise to read my book. Fortunately, she agreed to give me feedback. She helped me by editing parts of my book in a way that would be sensitive and helpful to those with mental health struggles. She was the perfect person to help in that way.

I was also blessed to have my dad, Randy McKnight, read through my book and offer editing advice. He is talented in technical writing and noticed mistakes I would not have noticed. I am grateful to him for providing his expertise and sacrificing his time on my behalf.

I am also indebted to my friends Camille Lindquist and Natalie Greaves who sacrificed time from their busy lives to read through my book and offer helpful advice and constructive criticism. I feel so fortunate to have so many talented people in my life who shared their writing and editing skills with me.

I received many confirmations from the Spirit during the writing process. I struggled with wording, trying to figure out how to describe a certain event or things I learned. Although it was usually an intense mental struggle with a lot of deleting and moving words around, eventually sentences would come together in a way that made sense.

In those moments when the words finally flowed and conveyed my thoughts just right, the Spirit would burn within my heart, confirming to me that I had received help and guidance from a higher power, assisting me to compose with a clear and focused mind. I gained a strong testimony of the Holy Ghost's ability to teach, enlighten, and bring things to my remembrance. The Spirit testified so strongly to me in those moments. Tears would flow with joy in knowing that God loved me enough to help me with a task that, although monumental to me, was menial in the grand scheme of things.

The writing process was such an emotional, mental, and spiritual feat. One night I logged onto my son's laptop I had been using and found that my book was unretrievable. Although I had emailed the book to myself a couple of days previously as a back-up, I realized my recent paragraphs I had composed would not be included on that.

I started to cry as I thought of the intense thought and emotional toil that had gone into writing those few paragraphs. I could not imagine being able to recreate those in the same way. Feeling frantic, as soon as Spencer walked up the stairs in the morning, I asked if there was any way to retrieve my book. I cannot explain the amount of relief I felt when he helped me find a copy that had been automatically saved to my email account.

That just confirmed to me how grueling and intense my emotional investment in the writing was. I could not stand the thought of needing to go through that process again even with a few of the paragraphs, especially ones that seemed to come together so perfectly with the help of the Spirit.

Sometimes inspiration came when I least expected it. For example, one day I was driving to the store when I started thinking about a personal experience. Specific wording came to mind that connected that experience to a scripture story I planned to share in my book. I did not want to take that inspiration for granted, so I immediately pulled the car over and wrote down those ideas.

When I returned home, I was able to add those thoughts from my phone to my book. The two stories combined perfectly to teach a powerful concept. Again, I saw a small miracle materialize before my eyes. The Spirit had guided my thoughts, making my book more meaningful.

I learned from that experience to jot down thoughts immediately as they came to me. I started keeping a notes page on my phone for all the random ideas and thoughts that I received during the day. I believe that God gives us more inspiration if He knows we will immediately act on the revelation we receive.

The biggest miracle happened when I was nearing the completion of the book. I had written all I felt inspired to include, but I wanted to go to the Lord again in prayer to see if there was anything else He wanted me to add. I had seen His hand in the process so much already that I knew He would let me know if there was anything the book was lacking. I decided I wanted to give my best effort to receive revelation from God, so I fasted, prayed, and went to the temple with an open mind and heart.

I got to the temple and wondered how God could direct me regarding my book, especially since I could not bring my book with me to look at for reference. God immediately demonstrated His ability to guide me. I sat down for the session and was filled with peace that only the serenity of the temple can bring. Within minutes, thoughts flowed to my mind.

My first thought was that I needed to incorporate the painting analogy into my book more. I realized I mainly talked about the analogy only in the introduction and conclusion. I knew I needed to tie it in better throughout the book. That immediate revelation took me by surprise. I knew those thoughts were from a higher power.

Then ideas started to flow as I thought of ways to incorporate the analogy. One of the ideas was to make all the chapter headings art related rather than the random titles I had. I was amazed at the clearness of my mind during that hour at the temple. I could remember the chapters of my book and was able to think through ideas of headings for them. Ideas continued to flow that I knew would add dimension to my book in a way I would not have thought of myself.

I did not imagine that the direction from my Heavenly Father would come so openly and clearly. From the time I sat down for the session to when I stood up to leave was a conduit of revelation. I was amazed at the ability of the Holy Ghost to teach me and to direct my thoughts. I had been working on my book for so long, but when I made the extra effort to include the Lord in the process, He blessed me in ways I did not know possible.

I am so grateful for the spiritual experiences I had while writing this book. My testimony grew as I recognized a strong heavenly connection throughout the process. I felt a burning in my heart repeatedly, testifying that the grace of the Savior gave me power beyond my own.

Because of the Atonement of Jesus Christ, I moved my personal mountain that seemed insurmountable. I know if I follow God's promptings, He will manifest His power in miraculous ways.

CITATIONS

4. ARTISTIC INFLUENCES

1. The Book of Mormon, Ether 6:7

5. BLEEDING COLORS

1. "FDA Pregnancy Categories." Drugs.com. https://www.drugs.com/pregnancy-categories.html

6. HIDDEN LAYERS

1. Fellowship Bible Church, "Glasses of Empathy," 2005, Little Rock, AR

9. EMERGING BEAUTY

1. D. Todd Christofferson, "Justification and Sanctification," *Ensign*, June 2001, 25
2. Dallin H. Oaks, "The Challenge to Become," *Ensign* or *Liahona*, November 2000, 30
3. Linda S. Reeves, "Claim the Blessings of Your Covenants," *Ensign* or *Liahona*, November 2013, 119
4. Reeves, "Claim the Blessings," 119

10. GOD'S TECHNIQUES

1. Bible Dictionary, s.v. "Grace," 697
2. Dictionary.com. https://www.dictionary.com/browse/enable
3. Sheri Dew, *Amazed by Grace* (Salt Lake City, Utah: Deseret Book Company, 2015), © Sheri Dew, Used by Permission of Deseret Book Company, 5-7
4. Brad Wilcox, "His Grace is Sufficient," BYU devotional address, 12 July 2011
5. Anthony Perkins, "Remember Thy Suffering Saints, O Our God," *Liahona*, November 2021, 104

6. The Book of Mormon, Mosiah 24:14
7. David A. Bednar, "Bear Up Their Burdens with Ease," *Ensign* or *Liahona*, May 2013, 88-89
8. Bednar, "Bear Up Their Burdens," 88-89
9. The Book of Mormon, Mosiah 24:15; emphasis added

11. FINDING THE MASTER PAINTER

1. Doctrine and Covenants 93:16
2. A Child's Prayer © 1984 Janice Kapp Perry. Used by permission.
3. KJV Bible, Matthew 27:46
4. S. Michael Wilcox, *When Your Prayers Seem Unanswered* (Salt Lake City, Utah: Deseret Book Company, 2006), © S. Michael Wilcox, Used by Permission of Deseret Book Company, 7-13
5. KJV Bible, Mark 6:45-46
6. KJV Bible, Mark 6:47
7. KJV Bible, Matthew 14:24
8. KJV Bible, Mark 6:48
9. S. Michael Wilcox, *When Your Prayers Seem Unanswered* (Salt Lake City, Utah: Deseret Book Company, 2006), © S. Michael Wilcox, Used by Permission of Deseret Book Company, 7-13
10. Macayle Stucki (@macaylestucki). "Neither of my girls learned to crawl." Instagram, March 13, 2022 https://www.instagram.com/p/Cb-DwNe7udrl/?utm_source=ig_web_copy_link
11. M. Russell Ballard, "Stay in the Boat and Hold On!," *Ensign* or *Liahona*, November 2014, 90-91
12. Juventa Vezzani, "Finding My Way through Mists of Darkness," *Ensign*, January 2016, 77
13. Vezzani, "Finding My Way," 77

12. ACCESSING THE SAVIOR'S PALETTE

1. Parson, Del, "Jesus at the Door (Jesus Knocking at the Door)."
2. KJV Bible, Matthew 14:28
3. Gene R. Cook, "Receiving Divine Assistance through the Grace of the Lord," *Ensign*, May 1993, 80
4. KJV Bible, Matthew 14:28
5. Compiled by Jerreld L. Newquist, Gospel Truth Volume 1: Discourses and Writings of George Q. Cannon (Salt Lake City, Utah: Deseret Book Company, 1974), © Jerreld L. Newquist, Used by Permission of Deseret Book Company, 147
6. Gene R. Cook, "Receiving Divine Assistance through the Grace of the Lord," *Ensign*, May 1993, 80

7. Bible Dictionary, s.v. "Prayer," 753

13. ETERNAL RULES OF COMPOSITION

1. Neil L. Andersen, "Power in the Priesthood," *Ensign* or *Liahona*, November 2013, 92
2. Russell M. Nelson, "The Temple and Your Spiritual Foundation," *Liahona*, November 2021, 94
3. KJV Bible, Matthew 11:29-30
4. Emily Belle Freeman, *Even This: Getting To The Place Where You Can Trust God With Anything*, (United States of America: Ensign Peak, 2017), © Emily Belle Freeman, Used by Permission of Deseret Book Company, 66
5. Freeman, *Even This*, 77
6. Doctrine and Covenants 82:10; italics added
7. Rex T. Young, *Diary of a Caregiver*, The Dementia Journey (Canton, MA: Author Reputation Press LLC, 2021), 110
8. Young, *Diary of a Caregiver*, 110
9. The Book of Mormon, Mosiah 24
10. The Book of Mormon, Mosiah 24:13

14. EMBRACING GOD'S METHODS

1. KJV Bible, Matthew 26:39
2. Richard G. Scott, "Trust in the Lord," *Ensign*, November 1995
3. Carol Wilkinson, "Becoming and Overcoming," BYU devotional address, 17 March 2009
4. Neal A. Maxwell, "Swallowed Up in the Will of the Father," *Ensign*, November 1995, 24

15. SAVORING THE CREATIVE PROCESS

1. Thomas S. Monson, "Finding Joy in the Journey," *Ensign* or *Liahona*, November 2008, 85
2. Thomas S. Monson, "Finding Joy in the Journey," *Ensign* or *Liahona*, November 2008, 87
3. Dieter F. Uchtdorf, "Grateful in Any Circumstances," *Ensign* or *Liahona*, May 2014, 76
4. The Book of Mormon, 1 Nephi 18:16
5. Dieter F. Uchtdorf, "Grateful in Any Circumstances," *Ensign* or *Liahona*, May 2014, 76

6. Viktor E. Frankl, *Man's Search for Meaning*, (Boston: Beacon Press, 2014), 62

16. JUST ENOUGH PAINT

1. Kate B. Carter, *Our Pioneer Heritage* (1975), 17:305
2. "How Firm a Foundation," *Hymns*, no. 85

17. DEPTH THROUGH SHADOWS

1. James E. Faust, "The Refiner's Fire," *Ensign*, May 1979, 53

18. ANGELIC LUSTER

1. Jeffrey R. Holland, "The Ministry of Angels," *Ensign* or *Liahona*, November 2008, 30
2. Holland, "The Ministry of Angels," 30

19. ARTISTIC INTERPRETATION

1. "Cleveland Clinic: Every Life Deserves World Class Care," https://my-clevelandclinic.org/health/drugs/15629-aspirin-sensitivity–aspirin-desensitization

20. ADDING DIMENSION

1. Doctrine and Covenants 122:9
2. The Book of Mormon, 2 Nephi 31:20

21. HIS MASTERPIECE

1. KJV Bible, Luke 8:46
2. KJV Bible, Luke 8:48
3. Jeffrey R. Holland, "Teaching and Learning in the Church," *Ensign*, June 2007, 95
4. Doctrine and Covenants 121:42
5. Neal A. Maxwell, "But for a Small Moment," BYU devotional address, 1 September 1974

6. The Mathnawi of Jalalu'ddin Rumi (1925-40), trans. Reynold A. Nicholson, vol. 5, 132), (as cited in L. Todd Budge, "Consistent and Resilient Trust," *Ensign* or *Liahona*, November 2019, 47
7. KJV Bible, Philippians 4:13